The Cambodian Crisis and U.S. Policy Dilemmas

The Cambodian Crisis and U.S. Policy Dilemmas

Robert G. Sutter

238066

Westview Press
BOULDER • SAN FRANCISCO • OXFORD

Westview Special Studies on South and Southeast Asia

This Westview softcover edition is printed on acid-free paper and bound in library-quality, coated covers that carry the highest rating of the National Association of State Textbook Administrators, in consultation with the Association of American Publishers and the Book Manufacturers' Institute.

Copyright © 1991 by Westview Press, Inc.

Published in 1991 in the United States of America by Westview Press, Inc., 5500 Central Avenue, Boulder, Colorado 80301, and in the United Kingdom by Westview Press, 36 Lonsdale Road, Summertown, Oxford OX2 7EW

Library of Congress Cataloging-in-Publication Data
Sutter, Robert G.
   The Cambodian crisis and U.S. policy dilemmas/Robert G. Sutter.
   p. cm.—(Westview special studies on South and Southeast Asia)
   Includes index.
   ISBN 0-8133-8047-2
   1. Cambodia—Politics and government—1975-   . 2. United States—
Foreign relations—Cambodia. 3. Cambodia—Foreign relations—
United States. 4. United States—Foreign relations—Vietnam.
5. Vietnam—Foreign relations—United States. 6. United States—
Foreign relations—1989-   . I. Title.
DS554.8.S87 1991
327.730596—dc20   90-13015
                                                            CIP

Printed and bound in the United States of America

The paper used in this publication meets the requirements
of the American National Standard for Permanence of Paper
for Printed Library Materials Z39.48-1984.

10   9   8   7   6   5   4   3   2   1

Contents

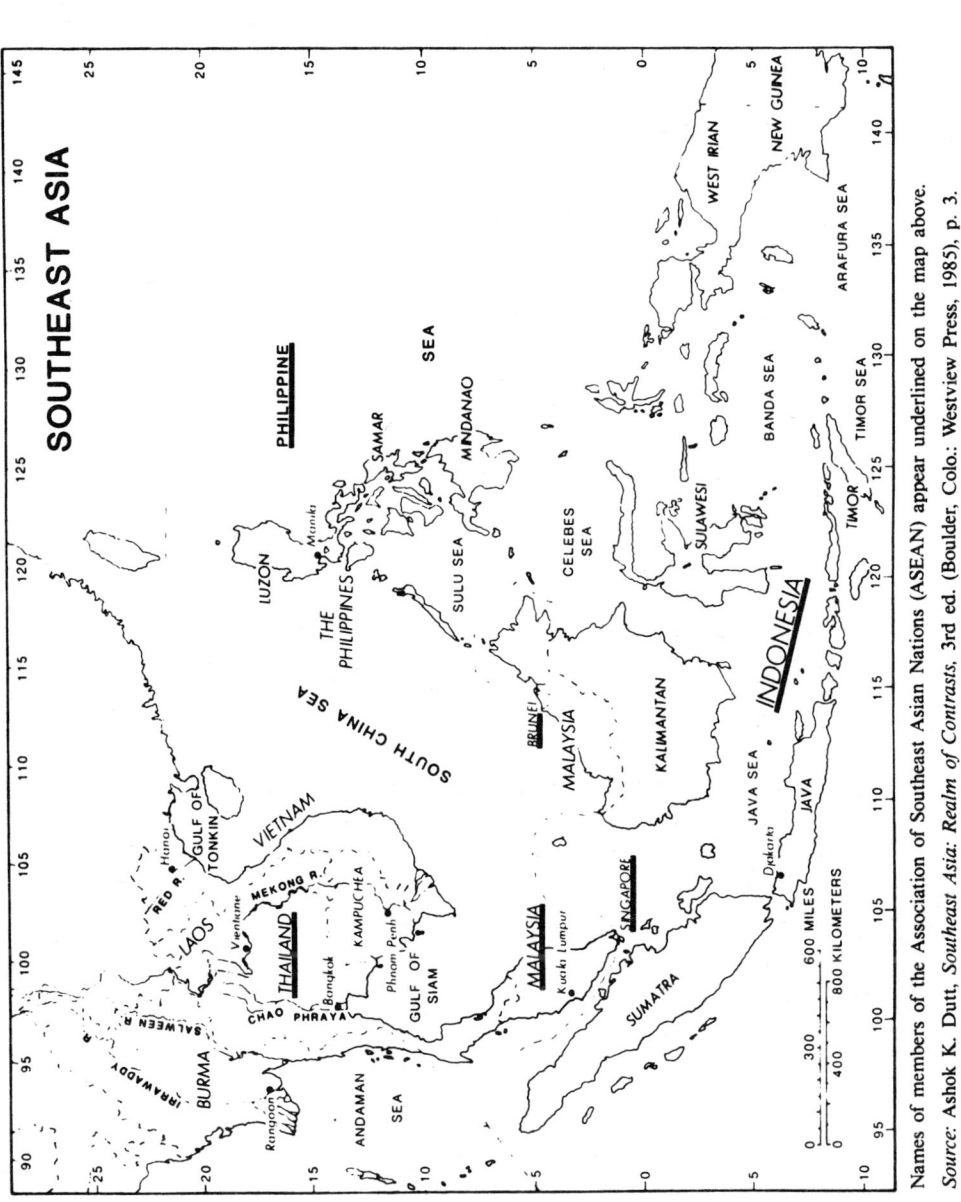

SOUTHEAST ASIA

Names of members of the Association of Southeast Asian Nations (ASEAN) appear underlined on the map above.

Source: Ashok K. Dutt, *Southeast Asia: Realm of Contrasts*, 3rd ed. (Boulder, Colo.: Westview Press, 1985), p. 3.

1

Introduction[1]

By 1990, the decade-long conflict in Cambodia caused by Vietnamese military occupation of the country had entered a new stage, and negotiations for a peace agreement had become more active. Vietnam withdrew most if not all its forces from Cambodia. Vietnamese officials and representatives of its client government in Phnom Penh expressed some flexibility regarding a compromise political settlement of the Cambodian conflict. This was strongly encouraged by their main international supporter, the Soviet Union. The three resistance groups (those led by the Khmer Rouge, Prince Sihanouk, and former Prime Minister Son Sann -- see Appendix C) and their main international backers in China, the Association of Southeast Asian Nations (ASEAN) -- see map, and the United States responded with varying degrees of flexibility.

All parties in the conflict appeared to see their interests as better served by making some adjustment in their positions, rather than by sticking to the intransigence of the previous 10 years. They held repeated deliberations, including an international conference on Cambodia that began in Paris July 30, 1989. But obstacles to a peace agreement remained. They centered on guaranteeing Vietnam's military withdrawal and achieving a peace agreement in Cambodia that would neither allow the return of the genocidal practices of the Khmer Rouge, nor permit Vietnam to continue domination over Cambodia.

U.S. policy faces dilemmas in Cambodia. Most notably the United States wants to help push back Vietnamese expansion in Indochina, and to support the positions of our treaty ally Thailand and other friends in ASEAN. But the United States strongly opposes the Khmer Rouge and fears that Vietnamese withdrawal may result in expanded scope for the Khmer Rouge and their brutal rule. In the past, U.S. policy dealt with these competing pressures by adopting a low posture that followed the lead of ASEAN. The United States has provided small amounts of nonlethal assistance to the two noncommunist resistance forces led by Prince Sihanouk and Son Sann, but it has refused any support to the third and most powerful member of the resistance groups, the Khmer Rouge. As the Vietnamese began to withdraw and the search for a peace agreement intensified, U.S. policymakers in the Bush administration and Congress proposed steps to strengthen the two noncommunist resistance groups led by Sihanouk and Son Sann, to block the return to power of the Khmer Rouge, and to relieve human suffering in Cambodia.

But U.S. policymakers strongly disagree about what steps are appropriate to reach these goals and support broader foreign policy objectives. Policy issues facing them at the start of the 1990s include the following:

- What are the most effective means for the United States to follow in order to curb the supply of weapons to the Khmer Rouge, or to otherwise insure that these Cambodian communists are not allowed to return to a dominant position of power in Cambodia?

- Should the United States strengthen the influence of the two noncommunist resistance forces that maintain a loose alignment with the Khmer Rouge against the Vietnamese-backed communist government in Phnom Penh?

- What is the effect on U.S. influence in the Cambodian situation of the absence of normal U.S. relations with Vietnam? What are the pros and cons of normalizing relations with Hanoi and what are the main procedures that would have to be considered in such normalization of relations?

- What is the appropriate U.S. policy toward China, the Soviet Union, Japan and other powers in regard to a Cambodian settlement? Is there possible common ground among them that could help to foster a settlement that would be in the interests of the United States? Is the United Nations or some other forum appropriate for these powers to meet to discuss Cambodia?

- How do U.S. policy interests in a Cambodian settlement and possible normalization of relations with Vietnam fit in with broad U.S. economic and humanitarian concerns including resolution of longstanding interests over U.S. prisoners of war and missing in action (POWs/MIAs) from the Vietnam War and the large refugee populations coming from Vietnam and Cambodia?

Current U.S. Interests Regarding
Cambodia and Vietnam

The collapse of the U.S.-supported governments in Phnom Penh and Saigon in 1975 marked the end of the U.S. role, begun in the 1950s, as the major foreign actor in Indochina. Under terms of the Nixon doctrine begun in 1969, the United States had already withdrawn U.S. combat troops from mainland Asia (with the notable exception of Korea) and had made clear to U.S. allies and associates that they would bear more responsibility for their own defense. Nevertheless, the United States has continued to maintain important political-strategic and humanitarian interests, and lesser economic concerns, in relations with Cambodia and Vietnam. U.S. policy in this area also is particularly sensitive because of the deep impact which the Vietnam War has had on American society and on the lives of several million U.S. servicemen and their families.

America's current political-strategic interests center on assuring a settlement in Cambodia that restores stability to Southeast Asia, secures the interests of our treaty ally Thailand and the other members of ASEAN, and checks the expansion of Soviet influence--through Vietnam or other means--in Southeast Asia. Such stability has been seen as unlikely to be restored under a peace agreement that allows the Vietnamese to continue to dominate Cambodia through its client, the PRK (also known as the "State of Cambodia") or other means; or one that allows the Khmer Rouge significantly to expand its power and re-establish draconian rule in the country.

The United States has a strong interest in the strategically and economically important communication routes that converge at the Straits of Malacca and other passageways in the region. The Soviet presence at U.S.-built bases in Vietnam--including Soviet bombers, fighter aircraft, submarines, and surface warships--has at times posed a potentially serious challenge to U.S. access to those routes,[2] but in late 1989, Moscow pulled back some forces from bases in Vietnam.[3] U.S. interest in working with ASEAN members to check Soviet-backed Vietnamese expansion proceeded in parallel with U.S. cooperation with other Asian regional actors concerned with Soviet and Vietnamese influence, notably China and Japan. Indeed, common opposition to suspected Soviet expansion or "hegemonism" in Asia was a central feature of U.S.-Chinese negotiations following President Nixon's opening to Beijing in 1972.

American humanitarian interests focus on prompting Vietnam to fully account for U.S. MIAs; facilitate orderly emigration procedures for Vietnamese relatives of U.S. residents and citizens, including children fathered by U.S. servicemen prior to 1975; release from detention and allow to emigrate Vietnamese associated with the U.S.-backed government of South Vietnam; and create measures to avoid the large-scale outflow of Vietnamese citizens in dangerously ill-equipped boats who fall prey to pirate atrocities, starvation, and other suffering. In Cambodia, humanitarian concerns for the well-being of the Cambodian people prompt the United States to press for international and other measures that would curb the power of the Khmer Rouge as the United States and other nations continue to urge a complete Vietnamese withdrawal.

U.S. economic interests are modest but include the possibility of developing trade and resources, such as off-shore oil, in Vietnam. A more immediate economic concern is to avoid having to pay a high price for restoration of normal relations with Phnom Penh or Hanoi. In particular, the U.S. government opposes past Vietnamese demands for several billion dollars in U.S. war reparations to Vietnam.

U.S. policy toward Vietnam also strives to avoid exacerbating past acrimonious debate over the war and where possible to reconcile the wide range of impulses and views within the United States regarding the Vietnam War. Those often contradictory impulses and views include the following:

- Continuing bitterness and hostility toward an enemy who killed over 50,000 Americans, has been slow in accounting for the U.S. MIAs, and is suspected by some in the United States of holding some live POWs.

- The desire for reconciliation with a former enemy.

- Unresolved attitudes about the issues and impact of the war, and a disposition on the part of some Americans, with the passage of time, to move on to new items on the national agenda.[4]

The recent interest of U.S. policymakers in a more assertive American role in Indochina marks a change from the relatively passive role adopted by the United States in the region following the defeat of U.S.-backed regimes in Saigon and Phnom Penh in 1975. It also reflects the changing realities of international power affecting Southeast Asia. In particular, the communist regimes in Moscow, Beijing and Hanoi have all become increasingly preoccupied in recent years with internal difficulties, and have been unable or unwilling to pursue the heretofore hardline policies that had made for a protracted impasse over the Cambodian conflict during most of the 1980s. In the newly fluid situation, the United States is able to exert more influence and its support is widely sought after by various competing actors in the Cambodian conflict.

In view of this changed situation, there is a need for basic information and analysis to assist the general American public in assessing the Cambodian crisis and its implications for U.S. interests. This brief study is designed to help meet some of that need. It is very much a synthetic work that relies heavily on and attempts to bring together the work of others in the field. As noted in footnotes below, it has made heavy use of available U.S. government reports and documents that are helpful in assessing Cambodian and Vietnamese developments and U.S. policy concerns. Chapter 1 introduces the current U.S. policy issues and interests concerning the crisis in Cambodia. Chapter 2 reviews the history of Cambodia, its recent foreign relations and the current state of the Cambodian economy and society. Chapter 3 provides an overview of the impasse in the Cambodian conflict that prevailed throughout much of the 1980s and assesses developments in the late 1980s that gave rise to the more fluid situation we face today. Chapter 4 looks in detail at U.S. policy concerns in both Cambodia and Vietnam. Chapter 5 concludes the study with a brief assessment of the likelihood of a more prominent U.S. leading role in policy toward Cambodia and Vietnam.

The study has several appendices and supporting materials. Appendix A provides a guide to the key leaders among the four competing factions in Cambodia. Appendix B examines at length procedural and jurisdictional questions that would be addressed if and when the United States decided to normalize diplomatic or economic relations with Vietnam. There is a chronology of significant events since 1975, a guide to further reading, a chart giving the status of the military-political groups active in Cambodia, a chart noting the contending groups and their stance on a peace agreement as of early 1990, and a chart giving key indicators regarding Cambodia and Vietnam. A map of Southeast Asia appears before page one.

Notes

1. The views expressed in this monograph are those of the author and not necessarily those of the Congressional Research or the Library of Congress.

2. Also, U.S. investment in ASEAN has grown steadily from a level of about $10 billion in the mid-1980s and U.S. trade has grown to a point that ASEAN, taken as a unit, is among the top 10 trading partners of the United States.

3.   See, for instance, coverage of a January 19, 1990, Soviet announcement regarding a withdrawal of forces from Vietnam in the *New York Times*, January 20, 1990, p. A4.

4.   Some press reports interpreted in this light President Bush's reference to Vietnam in his January 20, 1989, Inaugural Address.

2

Background on Cambodia

Cambodia came prominently to the attention of U.S. policymakers in the early 1970s, when the United States actively supported the non-communist Lon Nol government against the communist Khmer Rouge insurgents. It again became an important issue after 1978, when a Soviet-backed Vietnamese invasion toppled the Khmer Rouge regime. Cambodia was the center of a protracted military conflict and political dispute that has eased only in the past few years.[1] As background to developments in the 1970s and 1980s that have affected the Cambodian crisis, this chapter gives a country profile of Cambodia, with separate sections on Cambodia's history, geography, people, economy, government and foreign relations.

History

As a small country with weak economic, military and political institutions that is surrounded by often hostile and more powerful neighbors, Cambodia has suffered for centuries from poor leadership and outside pressures.

The major high point in Cambodian history was the Angkor period at the end of the first millennium. By A.D. 802, according to Khmer records, Jayavarman II established what became the Angkor Empire, the greatest power in the region for nearly six centuries. Royal power was based on the ideology which held the monarch to be semidivine. Jayavarman II conquered the region around the Tonle Sap and moved his capital to a site near what was to become Angkor Wat. The Angkor epoch provided the word which apparently became the name of the country - a 10th century inscription refers to the Kings of "Kambuja." Angkor consolidated its power steadily, reuniting the territory of Chenla, a state that had ruled over the territory of present day Cambodia in the sixth century.

Under Suryavarman II (1112-ca. 1150) Angkor expanded through successful wars against the Kingdom of Champa (in present-day

Vietnam), the Annamese (northern Vietnam), and the Burmese. Suryavarman also developed an extensive irrigation system and built Angkor Wat, considered to be the greatest single architectural masterpiece in Southeast Asia. Suryavarman's reign was followed by a period of dynastic upheaval and foreign invasion. Champa sacked Angkor in 1177, but was eventually driven out by Jayavarman VII (1181-1215) under whose reign Angkor reached its greatest territorial extent and built the capital city of Angkor Thom.

Angkor entered a long period of decline after Jayavarman VII. Growing pressure from the Thai people who migrated from China and neglect of the irrigation system contributed to the decline. Theravada Buddhism replaced Hinduism as the national religion during this period. In the 14th century, an independent Thai Kingdom was founded, and in 1353, a Siamese army sacked Angkor Wat. Warfare continued, with the Siamese capturing Angkor Thom in 1431, after which it was abandoned as the capital. Despite brief periods of resurgence, Cambodia's decline continued under encroachment from the Siamese, Vietnamese, and Lao. In the 17th and 18th centuries, an expanding Vietnamese population had taken over the Mekong Delta region from Cambodia while the Siamese expanded into Khmer areas in the west. By the mid-18th century, Cambodia had been reduced to its approximate present borders and was under virtual joint Siamese-Vietnamese suzerainty.

During the 1850s, King Ang Duong requested French assistance to save Cambodia from dissolution but was rejected. In 1859, Ang Duong was succeeded by his son, Norodom, who resumed negotiations for French protection. France acquired suzerainty over Vietnam by treaty in 1862 and offered to establish a protectorate. Norodom accepted and was crowned King by the French resident in 1863. In 1867, France persuaded Siam to abandon its claim to Cambodia but allowed the Thai to keep Battambang and Siem Riep Provinces, which were not recovered until the Franco-Siamese Treaty of 1907.

France made little effort to develop Cambodia's economy, being mainly interested in the country as a source of rice and plantation crops for export and as a buffer against Siamese or British influence in Indochina. In 1884, King Norodom was forced to accept a more stringent treaty with France, which made Cambodia a virtual colony. This occasioned a revolt, led by one of Norodom's brothers, which the French put down only at considerable cost. Cambodia became part of the Indochina Union with Laos, Annam, Tonkin, and Cochin-China. When King Norodom died in 1904, his sons, at French instigation, were passed over and a brother, Sisowath, crowned as King. Sisowath was succeeded in 1927 by his son Sisowath Monivong. When Monivong died in 1941, the French considered his son, Monireth, too independent and selected instead a great-grandson of King Norodom, Prince Norodom Sihanouk, to become King.

World War II saw Japanese forces enter Cambodia in 1941. Japan permitted Vichy France to continue administering the country but forced France to cede Battambang and Siem Riep provinces to Thailand (as Siam was named in 1939). Japan dissolved the French colonial administration in early 1945, and King Sihanouk declared independence on March 12. An anti-colonial government was formed under Son Ngoc Thanh, but arriving allied troops deposed it in October. Son Ngoc Thanh was arrested and exiled to France, but many of his supporters escaped and formed the Khmer Issarak (Free Khmer) to fight for independence.

In January 1946, France recognized Cambodia as an autonomous kingdom within the French Union, but significant elements of Cambodian sovereignty remained in French hands. Thailand returned the two northwestern provinces taken at the start of World War II. In domestic politics, two main political parties emerged during elections for the National Assembly in December 1947: the Liberals, largely comprised of court officials, senior civil servants, and landowners; and the Democratic Party, which drew its membership from lower officials, teachers, and some Khmer Issarak followers. The Democratic Party won a large majority in the assembly, which rejected the draft constitution and passed its own, promulgated on May 6, 1947. The Democratic Party opposed the 1948 draft treaty establishing Cambodia as an associated state in the French Union because it still left important powers in French hands. With ratification blocked, King Sihanouk dissolved the assembly in September 1949 and signed the treaty.

The Khmer Issarak, assisted by the anti-French Viet Minh, continued its resistance to French influence, undermining King Sihanouk's position. The Democratic Party again won control in elections for the National Assembly in 1951, continuing its opposition to the King. In 1952, Son Ngoc Thanh returned, adding to the threat to the monarchy. In June, Sihanouk took direct control of the government, and in January 1953, he dissolved the National Assembly and declared martial law. He then made his father regent and left the country for self-imposed exile, refusing to return to Phnom Penh until Cambodia gained genuine independence. Sihanouk's actions hastened the French government's July 4, 1953 announcement of its readiness to "perfect" the independence and sovereignty of Cambodia (and Laos and Vietnam). Negotiations culminated on November 9, 1953 with full independence.

The Geneva Agreements

The plenary session of the Geneva Conference began May 8, 1954. Cambodia, Laos, and the State (later Republic) of Vietnam - the three Associated States - were participants along with France, China, the United States, the Democratic Republic of Vietnam, the USSR, and the United Kingdom. The Agreement on the Cessation of Hostilities in Cambodia of July 20, 1954, provided for a cease-fire, withdrawal of all foreign armed forces and military personnel, and the establishment of an International Control Commission - representatives of Canada, India, and Poland - to supervise its execution.

All participants, except the United States and the State of Vietnam, associated themselves (by voice) with the final declaration. The U.S. delegate stated that U.S. policy with regard to the Geneva agreements would be to refrain from the threat or the use of force to disturb the agreements and that the United States would view any renewal of aggression in violation of the agreements with grave concern and as seriously threatening international peace and security.

The Cambodian delegation agreed to the neutrality of the three Indochinese states but insisted on a provision in the cease-fire agreement that left the Cambodian government free to call for outside military assistance should the Viet Minh again threaten its territory, or should others do so.

Neutral Cambodia

Subsequent domestic politics in Cambodia saw Sihanouk try and fail to amend the constitution in 1955 to strengthen his own powers at the expense of the National Assembly. In March, he abdicated in favor of his father, Norodom Suramarit, and formed his own political party, Sangkum Reastr Niyum (People's Socialist Community), to contest the National Assembly elections. The opposition, led by the Democratic Party and the small, procommunist People's Party (Pracheachon), was badly defeated, and Prince Sihanouk became prime minister. Despite its large majority, renewed in 1958, the heterogenous Sangkum was unable to form an effective, stable government. In 1960, King Suramarit died. Sihanouk resigned as prime minister but did not resume the throne. In July, he became head of state of Cambodia, leaving the throne vacant.

The central element of Cambodian foreign policy during the 1950s and the 1960s was neutrality. Sihanouk announced the policy in 1955 and reaffirmed it in refusing to join the U.S.-backed Southeast Asia Treaty Organization. In September 1957, Cambodia enacted a law to define neutrality as noncommitment to a military alliance or ideological bloc. Cambodia's neutral policy and close relations with communist countries were unwelcome to its neighbors, Thailand and South Vietnam. Relations with Thailand were broken in 1958 and, though restored the following year, were again broken in 1961, remaining severed throughout the 1960s. Relations with South Vietnam were broken in 1963 over border violations by South Vietnamese forces and South Vietnam's support for Son Ngoc Thanh and his antimonarchist forces, now called the Khmer Serei.

By the mid-1960s, parts of Cambodia's eastern provinces were serving as bases for North Vietnamese army and Viet Cong (NVA/VC) forces operating against South Vietnam. The port of Sihanoukville (since renamed Kompong Som) was being used to supply them. As NVA/VC activity grew, the United States and South Vietnam became increasingly concerned. In 1969 the United States began a series of air raids against NVA/VC base areas.

Most organized opposition to Sihanouk had subsided after the 1958 elections but, as the 1960s continued, opposition to Prince Sihanouk's foreign policy and resentment of his increasingly autocratic rule resurfaced, both from the middle classes and from leftist groups. Paris-educated leftists such as Son Sen, Ieng Sary, and Saloth Sar (later known as Pol Pot), went into the countryside in the early 1960s, to lead an insurgency under the clandestine Communist Party of Kampuchea (CPK). In the 1966 National Assembly elections, Sihanouk permitted several candidates to run in each constituency under the Sangkum banner. The election resulted in a significant swing to the right, and a new government was formed under General Lon Nol. Sihanouk formed a shadow government in which many leftists were represented, including Khieu Samphan. Sihanouk blamed the leftist insurgents, whom he labelled the "Khmer Rouge" (literally "Red Khmer"), for a 1967 peasant uprising in Battambang province and ordered a massive crackdown. More leftist leaders such as Khieu Samphan now fled Phnom Penh to join the insurgency.

During 1968 and 1969, the insurgency worsened, and Prince Sihanouk became increasingly alarmed at the growing NVA/VC presence in the eastern part of the country. Popular anti-Vietnamese sentiment was also rising, fanned in part by the conservative opposition. Sihanouk's diplomatic efforts to persuade the Vietnamese to leave were unsuccessful. In August, Sihanouk asked General Lon Nol, who had resigned in 1967, to form a new government. The government, which included Sisowath Sirik Matak, a long-time opponent of Sihanouk, as deputy prime minister, began to exclude the prince from decisionmaking.

Under increasing pressure from conservatives in the National Assembly, Sihanouk left Cambodia in January 1970 for medical treatment in France. Anti-Vietnamese riots broke out in March in some eastern provinces and spread to Phnom Penh.

The Khmer Republic and the War

On March 18, 1970, Sihanouk was overthrown. The National Assembly voted to withdraw its confidence from the head of state, investing the speaker of the assembly with his powers, and, the following day, declared a state of emergency, giving full power to Prime Minister Lon Nol. Son Ngoc Thanh and his Khmer Serei announced their support for the new government. On October 9, the Cambodian monarchy was abolished, and the country renamed the Khmer Republic.

The Vietnamese rejected the government's request for the withdrawal of NVA/VC troops and began to reinfiltrate some of the 2,000-4,000 Cambodians who had gone to North Vietnam after the Geneva accord in 1954. They became cadre in the insurgency. Prince Sihanouk joined with the insurgents to form the Royal Government of the National Union of Kampuchea (RGNU) in exile in Beijing. The prestige of his name assisted the insurgents in attracting new recruits from the peasantry, but control of the movement rested with the CPK under the nominal leadership of Khieu Samphan.

The Khmer Republic government initially enjoyed broad support from the middle classes in the cities and towns and many thousands joined the expanding army, but much of the peasantry was politically apathetic or loyal to Prince Sihanouk. Peasants demonstrated in several areas in support of the prince. At the same time, the United States moved to provide material assistance to the new government's armed forces, which were engaged against both the Khmer Rouge insurgents and NVA/VC forces. In April, U.S. and South Vietnamese forces entered Cambodia in a campaign aimed at destroying NVA/VC base areas. A considerable quantity of equipment was seized or destroyed, but NVA/VC forces eluded American and South Vietnamese forces by moving deeper into Cambodia. NVA/VC units overran many Cambodian Army positions while the Khmer Rouge expanded their small-scale attacks on lines of communication.

The Khmer Republic's leadership was plagued by disunity among its three principal figures: Lon Nol, Sirik Matak, and National Assembly leader In Tam. Lon Nol remained in power in part because none of the others was prepared to take his place. In 1972, a new constitution was adopted and Lon Nol elected President. The Khmer Republic's first parliament was elected in August and September of that year. Disunity, the problems of transforming a 30,000-man army into a national combat force of more than 200,000 men, and spreading corruption weakened the civilian administration and army, draining the enthusiastic urban support so prominent just after Sihanouk's deposition.

The insurgency continued to grow, with supplies and military support provided by North Vietnam. Increasingly, however, the internal leadership under Pol Pot, Ieng Sary, and Khieu Samphan asserted its dominance over the Vietnamese-trained communists, many of whom were purged. At the same time, the Khmer Rouge forces became stronger and more independent of the Vietnamese. By 1973 the Khmer Rouge were fighting major battles with government forces on their own. They controlled nearly 60 percent of Cambodia's territory and 25 percent of its population. Concern about continued U.S. support began to affect government morale.

The Paris Accords of January 1973, which ended the direct U.S. combat role in the Vietnam War, moved the government to the first of three unsuccessful attempts to enter into negotiations with the insurgents. Lon Nol suspended offensive actions to enable the NVA/VC to withdraw. In July 1973 and again in July 1974, the government offered to open talks, but both Sihanouk and the communists refused the offers. By 1974, the Khmer Rouge were operating more boldly, as divisions, and virtually all combat NVA/VC forces had moved into South Vietnam. The Khmer Rouge controlled most of the countryside outside of enclaves around the cities and main transportation routes. More than two million refugees from the war lived in Phnom Penh and other cities.

On New Year's Day 1975, communist troops launched an offensive which, in 117 days of the hardest fighting in the war, destroyed the Khmer Republic. Simultaneous attacks around the perimeter of Phnom Penh pinned down republican forces, while other Khmer Rouge units overran fire bases controlling the vital lower Mekong River resupply route. Only one Mekong River convoy was able to reach Phnom Penh after the offensive began, and it was badly damaged. A U.S.-funded airlift of ammunition and rice ended when Congress refused additional aid for Cambodia. Phnom Penh and other cities were subjected to daily rocket attacks causing thousands of civilian casualties. Phnom Penh surrendered on April 17, five days after the U.S. Mission evacuated Cambodia.

Democratic Kampuchea

Many Khmer welcomed the arrival of peace, but the Khmer Rouge soon turned Kampuchea into a land of horror unequaled in modern history. Immediately after its victory, the new regime ordered the evacuation of all cities and towns, sending the entire population out into the countryside to till the land. Thousands starved or died of disease during the evacuation. Many of those forced to evacuate the cities were resettled in "new villages," which lacked provision for food or medical care. Many starved before the first harvest, and hunger and malnutrition bordering on starvation were constant during those years. Those who resisted or who questioned orders were immediately executed, as were most military and civil leaders of the former regime who failed to disguise their past.

Prince Sihanouk returned from exile with members of the RGNU, but the CPK held all significant power. Within the CPK, power rested with the Paris-educated leadership: Pol Pot, Ieng Sary, Khieu Samphan, and Son Sen. (See Appendix A for a guide to key leaders in Cambodia.) A new constitution in January 1976 established Democratic Kampuchea (DK) as a communist people's republic. A 250-member Assembly of the Representatives of the People of Kampuchea (PRA) was elected in March to choose the collective leadership of a State Presidium, whose chairman became the head of state. Sihanouk resigned as head of state on April 4, 1976, and RGNU Prime Minister Penn Nouth announced the resignation of the RGNU Cabinet April 6. On April 14, after its first session, the PRA announced that Khieu Samphan would chair the State Presidium for a five year term. It also picked a 15-member Cabinet headed by Pol Pot as prime minister. Prince Sihanouk was put under virtual house arrest.

The new government sought to completely restructure Kampuchean society. Remnants of the old society were abolished, Khmer literature and culture destroyed, and Buddhism suppressed. The regime controlled every aspect of life and reduced people to the level of abject obedience through terror. Public executions of those considered unreliable or discovered to have links with the previous government were common. Torture centers were established where detailed records were kept of the thousands murdered there. Few succeeded in fleeing the country or escaped the military patrols. Agriculture was collectivized, and the surviving part of the industrial base abandoned or placed under state control. Kampuchea had neither a national currency nor a banking system.

Solid estimates of the number who died between 1975 and 1979 are not available. Hundreds of thousands were probably executed by the regime, often in the most brutal manner. Hundreds of thousands more died of starvation and disease both during the Khmer Rouge period and after the dislocations caused by the Vietnamese invasion. Estimates of the dead range from 1.5 million to 3 million, out of a 1975 population estimated at 7.3 million.[2]

Democratic Kampuchea's relations with its neighbors, Vietnam and Thailand, worsened rapidly as a result of border clashes and ideological differences. The CPK was fiercely anti-Vietnamese, and most Khmer communists who had lived in Vietnam were purged. Democratic Kampuchea established close ties with China, and the Kampuchean-Vietnamese conflict became part of the Sino-Soviet rivalry with Moscow backing Vietnam. Border clashes worsened as Democratic Kampuchea Armed Forces attacked villages in Vietnam. By mid-1978, Vietnamese forces had retaliated by invading Kampuchea, advancing some 30 miles. The arrival of the rainy season brought a halt to the Vietnamese advance. Kampuchea broke relations with Vietnam and appealed for help to the United Nations.

In December, Vietnam announced formation of the Kampuchean United Front for National Salvation (KUFNS) under Heng Samrin, a former DK division commander. It was composed of Khmer Rouge officials like Heng Samrin who had fled Kampuchea in 1978 after a failed coup attempt against Pol Pot. On Christmas Day, 1978, Vietnamese forces launched a full invasion of Kampuchea, capturing Phnom Penh on January 7 and driving the remnants of Kampuchea's army toward its borders. Prince Sihanouk, released from house arrest by the Khmer Rouge, went to the United Nations to denounce Vietnam.

The Vietnamese Occupation

On January 10, 1979 the Vietnamese installed Heng Samrin as head of state in the new People's Republic of Kampuchea (PRK). The Vietnamese army continued its pursuit of Khmer Rouge forces under Pol Pot. Hundreds of thousands of Khmer displaced during the Pol Pot era and the Vietnamese invasion began streaming to the Thai border in search of refuge. The international community responded with a massive relief effort to prevent widespread starvation and disease among the Kampuchean people. The United Nations, through UNICEF and the World Food Program, coordinated relief efforts. More than $400 million was provided between 1979 and 1982, of which the United States contributed nearly $100 million. At one point more than 500,000 Khmer were living along the Thai-Kampuchean border and more than 100,000 more in holding centers inside Thailand.

Vietnam's 150,000-170,000-man occupation army controlled the major populations centers and most of the countryside. The Heng Samrin regime's own armed forces numbered 20,000-30,000 but were plagued by poor morale and widespread desertion. Resistance to Vietnam's occupation continued.

A large portion of the Khmer Rouge armed forces of Democratic Kampuchea eluded Vietnamese forces and established themselves in remote regions. The noncommunist resistance, consisting of a number of groups which had been fighting the Khmer Rouge since 1975 under the leadership of Lon Nol era soldiers, coalesced in 1979-80. They formed the Khmer People's National Liberation Armed Forces, which pledged loyalty to former Prime Minister Son Sann, and Moulinaka (Movement pour la Liberation Nationale de Kampuchea), loyal to Prince Sihanouk. In 1979, Son Sann formed the Khmer People's National Liberation Front (KPNLF) to lead the political struggle for Kampuchea's independence. Prince Sihanouk formed his own organization, FUNCINPEC, and its military arm, the Armee Nationale Sihanoukienne (ANS) in 1981. (See Appendix C for a chart giving status of the military-political groups active in Cambodia.)

Warfare followed a wet season-dry season rhythm in which the heavily armed Vietnamese forces conducted offensive operations during the dry season and the resistance forces had the initiative during the rainy season. In 1982, Vietnam launched a major offensive against the main Khmer Rouge base at Phnom Melai in the Cardamom Mountains in the southwestern part of the country but failed to capture it. Vietnam switched its target to civilian camps near the Thai border in 1983, launching a series of massive assaults, backed by armor and heavy artillery, against camps belonging to all three resistance groups. Hundreds of civilians were injured in these attacks and more than 80,000 civilians were forced to flee to Thailand. The resistance military forces, however, were largely undamaged.

By 1983, the resistance forces had all grown larger and more effective and challenged Vietnam's position with growing success. Khmer Rouge forces numbered some 35,000-40,000 men. The KPNLF had 13,000 armed men and 6,000 more awaiting arms. Prince Silhanouk's ANS had 4,000-5,000 men, with more unarmed. The 1983 rainy season saw a marked increase in the scope and intensity of resistance activity, a pattern which continued into the 1984 dry season in which resistance forces attacked Vietnamese occupied areas, including several provincial capitals.

Within Cambodia, the Vietnamese had only limited success in establishing their client Heng Samrin regime, which remained dependent on Vietnamese advisers. Security in some rural areas remained tenuous, and major transportation routes were subject to interdiction by resistance forces. A Vietnamese security crackdown against suspected resistance sympathizers in May and June 1983 drove nearly 20,000 additional refugees to flee to camps near the Thai border and further alienated the populace. The settlement of Vietnamese nationals in Kampuchea further exacerbated anti-Vietnamese sentiment. Reports of the numbers involved varied widely; some were returning former residents, but they included many new immigrants as well. The Vietnamese faced Khmer nationalism reasserting itself against the traditional Vietnamese enemy and an increasingly intractable military situation.

Geography, People, Economy, and Government

Geography

Cambodia is a land of rice paddies and forest-covered hills and mountains on the Southeast Asian peninsula. The flat central area, formed by the basin of the Mekong River and the Tonle Sap (Great Lake), provides ideal conditions for rice cultivation. A prominent escarpment, the Dangrek Range, runs along the Thai border on the north. A generally level plain, bounded by the Cardamom Mountains in the southwest and rising to hills and mountains along the Lao and Vietnamese borders, descends to a flood plain in the southeast. The coastline on the Gulf of Thailand is irregular, fronted by numerous offshore islands, some of which are inhabited. The highest point in Kampuchea, Phnom Aural in the Cardamom Mountains, rises 5,780 feet above the sea level.

Cambodia has a tropical monsoon climate with a dry season from November to May. Annual rainfall at Phnom Penh is approximately 58 inches (145 cm.). Year-round temperatures vary from about 20 degrees centigrade-36 degrees centigrade (68 degrees fahrenheit-97 degrees fahrenheit). Humidity is consistently high. December and January are the most comfortable months.

People

Population density in Cambodia is low compared with most Southeast Asian countries. The urban population increased sharply during the 1970-1975 war, but after seizing power, the Khmer Rouge forced nearly all urban residents to return to rural areas as peasants. Most of the urban population that survived the Khmer Rouge period subsequently fled. Few cities or towns have recovered to their 1970 populations.

About 90 percent of the people are ethnic Khmer, including Khmer Loeu. The Khmer Loeu are hill tribes (the "upper Khmer" to distinguish them from the "center Khmer" or Khmer Kandal of the ricelands and the "lower Khmer" or Khmer Krom, who live in Vietnam's Mekong Delta). Before 1975, the Chinese minority numbered several hundred thousand. Many of those who survived fled abroad as refugees. The Vietnamese minority, numbering 300,000-500,000 in 1970, suffered a pogrom during the early months of what later became the Khmer Republic. At that time, large numbers of

Vietnamese returned to South Vietnam. Nearly all who remained fled after the Khmer Rouge takeover in 1975. The Chams are Malayo-Polynesian Muslims descended for the most part from the people of the ancient Kingdom of Champa. A small Burmese minority exploited the gem deposits near Pailin before and during the war. The European, Thai, and Lao of earlier years left after the installation of a communist government.

Theravada Buddhism was the state religion in Cambodia until 1975 and the faith of the great majority of the Cambodian people. The Chams follow Islam, and some hill tribes are animist. All religion was suppressed between 1975 and 1979. It has since begun to be restored.

Cambodia's long tradition of rudimentary education for boys in monastery schools developed into an extensive government-run school network culminating in a university system for 10,000 students by the late 1960s. That system was destroyed under the Khmer Rouge. The Heng Samrin regime began to reestablish education in areas under its control. Rudimentary primary and middle schools exist in the civilian camps near the Thai border.

Refugees. Many Cambodians, particularly those who were part of the Khmer Republic government or armed forces, sought to flee their country after the Khmer Rouge victory in 1975. During the Khmer Rouge period, very few people were able to evade the tight controls and military patrols to escape but, after the Vietnamese invasion and the breakdown of the Khmer Rouge control, more than 700,000 people fled toward Thailand.

Thailand gave refuge to more than 220,000 before it closed its border with Cambodia in 1980. As many as 500,000 more Cambodians remained on the Cambodian side of the border where they were given assistance by U.N. and private voluntary agencies. More than 165,000 were accepted for resettlement abroad (more than 100,000 by the United States alone), and many voluntarily returned to Cambodia. Some Cambodians remain inside Thailand, awaiting offers of resettlement abroad. About 300,000 Cambodians continue to live in camps near the Thai border. The Royal Thai Government, the U.N. Border Relief Operation, the International Committee of the Red Cross, and private voluntary organizations work together to provide these people food and medical care. The United States has joined with other countries to provide assistance.

Economy

The economy is based on agriculture and related industries. Over the past decade Cambodia has been slowly recovering from its near destruction by war and political upheaval. It still remains, however, one of the world's poorest countries, with an estimated per capita GDP of under $100. The food situation is precarious; during the 1980s famine was averted only through international relief. In 1986 the production level of rice, the staple food crop, was able to meet only 80 percent of domestic needs. A success of the nation's recovery program has been in the new rubber plantings and in fishing. In 1985 small quantities of rubber were exported, and the fish catch came to 65,000 tons. Industry, other than rice processing, is only beginning. Foreign trade has been primarily with the USSR and Vietnam. Statistical data on the economy continues to be sparse and unreliable.

The cities and towns remain under-populated, although life has returned to Phnom Penh and some provincial capitals. Basic services, such as electricity and water, are erratic. The Heng Samrin government has attempted to restore the educational system and has announced great success in its literacy campaign. Health conditions remain poor.

Since the end of the 1979-1981 emergency period, Western aid to Cambodia has fallen off. Aid from the Soviet Union and Eastern Europe has been directed at basic infrastructure projects and has made little impact on the bulk of the population outside the towns. U.N. agencies such as UNICEF provide limited assistance. A number of private organizations are active in Cambodia.

Along the Thai-Cambodian border, the U.N. Border Relief Operation (UNBRO) coordinates relief efforts for the 300,000 Cambodians who remain near the border. In the mid-1980s, UNBRO spent about $30 million annually in relief efforts. The United States has been a major contributor to UNBRO.

Government

The People's Republic of Kampuchea (PRK) is a Vietnamese-style people's republic. The single party, the Kampuchean People's Revolutionary Party (KPRP), controls the government, and its Secretary General, Heng Samrin, is also Chairman of the State Presidium. At least until recently, however, real power, rested with Vietnam, which maintained advisers at every level of government who made or approved all major decisions. A national assembly was "elected" in 1981. All candidates were selected by the KPRP and approved by the Vietnamese. The regime restored the pre-1975 system of provinces but reduced the number to 18 by combining Siem Riep and Oddar Meanchey into a single province. A constitution was promulgated in 1981. In 1989, the government was reorganized and renamed the "State of Cambodia."

Although driven from Phnom Penh, the Khmer Rouge government of Democratic Kampuchea continued to function after 1979 in areas it controlled near the Thai border. Pol Pot was replaced as leader of the regime by Khieu Samphan but continued to serve as commander in chief of its army, the National Army of Democratic Kampuchea. The Khmer Rouge have made an effort to convince the Cambodian people that they have changed their policies. Buddhism has been revived and private agriculture encouraged. The Khmer Rouge remain, however, a society controlled thoroughly from the top. In 1981 the Communist Party of Kampuchea was formally dissolved, although most observers believe it continued as the clandestine organization it was before 1975.

In June 1982, the members of the Association of Southeast Asian Nations (ASEAN) promoted agreement between the Khmer Rouge and the two principal noncommunist resistance groups, the KPNLF and FUNCINPEC, to form a loose coalition. The newly formed Coalition Government of Democratic Kampuchea (CGDK) included Prince Sihanouk as president and chief of state, Son Sann as prime minister and head of government, and Khieu Samphan as vice president for foreign affairs. (See Appendix C for chart giving the status of the military-political groups active in Cambodia.) The 1976 constitution was no longer in effect. Four coordinating committees -- defense, finance and economy, culture and education, and health and social affairs -- acted as ministries with representatives from each group. Each faction remained autonomous, administering civilian camps loyal to it and maintaining its own armed forces. The coalition was organized to coordinate resistance efforts and support implementation of a solution to the Cambodian problem.

Foreign Relations

The Coalition Government of Democratic Kampuchea has formal diplomatic relations at the ambassadorial level with China, North Korea, and some Third World countries. A number of other governments, including Japan and some European countries, formally recognized Democratic Kampuchea after 1975 and have never withdrawn their recognition. The coalition also represents Cambodia at the United Nations, where successive Vietnamese-inspired challenges to Democratic Kampuchea's credentials were defeated.

The Phnom Penh regime has exchanged ambassadors with Vietnam, Laos, the USSR, several East European countries, and India. It claimed recognition by a total of 30 governments or liberation movements. The withdrawal of Vietnamese forces and adoption of more flexible economic policies improved the PRK's international standing. Most notably, in 1990 the Thai prime minister was in the forefront of those wishing to end the conflict and to strengthen mutually beneficial economic relations with Phnom Penh.

ASEAN has led international opposition to Vietnam's invasion and occupation of Cambodia. The 1981 U.N.-sponsored international conference on Cambodia brought together 83 countries as participants or observers. The conference declaration called for the withdrawal of all foreign forces and the restoration of Cambodian independence and self-determination through internationally supervised elections. This formula for a settlement was included in successive U.N. General Assembly resolutions since 1979 which were adopted by large majorities, including the United States, Japan, China, Western Europe, and the majority of nonaligned nations.

While insisting on the central elements of the international conference formula, complete withdrawal and self-determination, the ASEAN countries have been flexible in their approach to Cambodia. They have made several initiatives designed to provide for a comprehensive political settlement, while addressing the security concerns of all Cambodia's neighbors. The 1983 ASEAN "Appeal on Kampuchea" suggested a phased withdrawal of Vietnamese troops, coupled with an international peacekeeping force and assistance to reconstruct areas evacuated by Vietnam. Until recently, Hanoi rejected such proposals, calling instead for regional talks on peace and security in Southeast Asia. Such talks appeared to be designed to put off discussion of the Cambodian problem by linking it to other security issues. For a long time, Vietnamese proposals ignored the underlying issue of Vietnam's occupation, dealt with the matter as only a security problem along the Thai-Cambodian border, and sought recognition for the Phnom Penh regime.

Notes

1. For additional background on Cambodia, see Suggested Readings, below. Much of the information and presentation in this section relies heavily on the discussion seen in "Kampuchea (Cambodia)," Background Notes, U.S. Department of State, Bureau of Public Affairs, May 1984: 10pp.

2. This evaluation of these estimates is taken from the U.S. government report noted above. For other estimates, see Suggested Readings below.

3

Evolution of the Cambodian Problem in the 1980s

The Cambodian Impasse

The Vietnamese military invasion of Cambodia on Christmas Day 1978 precipitated a major international crisis and led to prolonged military stalemate in Cambodia and international confrontation in Southeast Asia and at the United Nations. Vietnam faced major disputes with the xenophobic Khmer Rouge regime and feared China's intentions in backing the Khmer Rouge and its firm stance on other Sino-Vietnamese issues. Vietnam decided to tilt to the Soviet side of the Sino-Soviet split. Signing a formal friendship treaty with Moscow gave Vietnam the international support it needed before resorting to direct military invasion in order to secure its interests in Cambodia. Vietnam installed a client regime (the People's Republic of Kampuchea - PRK -- known later as the "State of Cambodia") led by dissident Khmer Rouge cadre, backed it with the fire power of over 100,000 Vietnamese troops, and secured the main cities, towns and lines of communications. While world opinion generally welcomed the overthrow of the bloody Khmer Rouge, who were responsible for over one million deaths while in power from 1975 to 1979, it roundly condemned the Vietnamese military invasion.

The Khmer Rouge fighters, strongly backed by China, continued to resist from bases along the Thai-Cambodian border. Gradually, separate noncommunist resistance forces under the leadership of former head of state Prince Sihanouk and former prime minister Son Sann also emerged and received material support from the Association of Southeast Asian Nations (ASEAN), China, and the United States. The three resistance groups were often at odds with one another, but they remained loosely connected in a coalition government that was widely recognized and continued to occupy Cambodia's seat in the United Nations. (See Appendix C for a list of Cambodian groups).

China conducted a month-long limited invasion inside Vietnam in early 1979 "to teach the Vietnamese a lesson," and Beijing subsequently maintained several hundred thousand troops along Vietnam's northern border. China, ASEAN, and the West placed restrictions on economic and diplomatic interaction with Vietnam until it withdrew its forces from Cambodia.

Vietnam intensified the military conflict in Cambodia with a major offensive in 1984-85 that succeeded in destroying a number of the resistance forces' bases along the Thai border; and it attempted to seal the border against infiltration. The offensive was only a temporary success as the resistance forces received strong material and political support from China and ASEAN, regrouped their fighters, and began new actions inside Cambodia.

The balance of military, political and other forces affecting the Cambodian situation in the mid-1980s gave little cause for optimism about significant change anytime soon. Each of the principal protagonists in the stalemate appeared determined to pursue existing policies. All seemed convinced that they had vital interests at stake and that conceivable alternatives to existing polices were adverse to those interests.[1]

Vietnam's aged leadership demonstrated the same determination that enabled them to defeat both the French and the Americans. Hanoi appeared prepared to continue to endure the negative consequences of war and isolation stemming from the Vietnamese occupation of Cambodia. Results of the invasion and occupation included an exchange of the enmity of the United States for that of China, and the loss of considerable international standing. However, the Vietnamese had succeeded in stabilizing to a considerable extent their Cambodian flank. This was better than the dangers they saw in a Cambodia led by Pol Pot and backed by a threatening China. While claiming that the situation in Cambodia was "irreversible," Vietnamese officials stressed that they could not remove their troops from Cambodia until China ended its aggressive stance.

As the main international backer of Vietnam and its client, the PRK, the Soviet Union was viewed with suspicion throughout non-communist Southeast Asia. Cambodia also had become a major regional "hot spot" serving to exacerbate tensions in Moscow's relations with Beijing. But a major benefit for Moscow was increased Soviet military access to air and naval bases in Vietnam. From Cam Ranh Bay, Soviet naval forces can reach the Indian Ocean in half the time it takes from Vladivostok. Use of Vietnamese facilities helped the Soviets maintain a continuous naval presence in the South China Sea. It also improved Soviet ability to collect intelligence on China and on the United States and its allies.

Opposed to the PRK-Vietnamese-Soviet coalition were the three loosely unified Cambodian resistance groups backed by China, ASEAN, and the United States. Beijing's position was in part a manifestation of longstanding Sino-Vietnamese hostility which has deep historical roots. The hostility was exacerbated by the overlay of the Sino-Soviet conflict in Southeast Asia as Hanoi moved closer to Moscow to secure its position vis-a-vis an increasingly threatening China prior to Vietnamese invasion of Cambodia in December 1978. Beijing's decision in early 1978 to put aside its past efforts to sustain some balance in its relations with Vietnam came as a result of numerous problems and perceived Vietnamese provocations. The disagreements centered on disputes over the land border, competing claims to the Paracel and Spratly Islands in the South China Sea, Vietnam's persecution of overseas Chinese in Vietnam, and Hanoi's increasingly close relationship with Beijing's prime security threat, the USSR.[2]

The Vietnamese became convinced that hostile Chinese intent lay behind Beijing's close ties with the Khmer Rouge. Hanoi charged Beijing with using Cambodia as an instrument of its own aggressive policy against Vietnam. In response, Hanoi sought the strategic guarantee provided by a security alliance and close military relationship with the USSR. This action merely increased Beijing's concern that Vietnam was a willing accomplice in the perceived Soviet effort to surround, isolate and ultimately intimidate China in Asia.

The rapid collapse of the Khmer Rouge in the face of the Vietnamese assault was a severe blow to China's interest. And Chinese forces did not do particularly well in their efforts to teach Vietnam a lesson during the Chinese military incursion into northern Vietnam in February-March 1979. Nevertheless, Beijing sustained military pressure along Vietnam's northern border, supplied generous aid to the Khmer Rouge insurgents who regrouped along the Thai border, gave some aid to the two noncommunist Cambodian resistance groups, built an increasingly strong military relationship with Thailand, and remained ever vigilant in shoring up firm international opposition to the Vietnamese occupation of Cambodia.

Reflecting a range of opinion among the member states, ASEAN's position was less demanding than China's but no less persistent in pressing for the withdrawal of all foreign forces and for self-determination for the Cambodian people without outside interference. The ASEAN countries were careful to note Vietnam's legitimate concerns. They acknowledged Vietnam's particular interest in Cambodia and the fact that Pol Pot's extremism was indeed partly responsible for the aggravation of relations leading to Vietnam's invasion. Although the ASEAN countries campaigned for the Khmer Rouge regime, Democratic Kampuchea, to continue to occupy the Cambodian seat at the U.N., they repeatedly made clear their opposition to Pol Pot and the Khmer Rouge. In 1982 ASEAN helped implement the coalition government (the CGDK -- see Appendix C) under Prince Sihanouk, partly to prevent the annual embarrassment of supporting Pol Pot and partly as a means of strengthening the noncommunist opposition. The belief was that the noncommunist opposition, if it grew in strength, could become the basis for a future political solution in Cambodia. Otherwise the situation was seen as likely to boil down to a choice between the Vietnamese-backed communist PRK and the Chinese-backed communist Khmer Rouge.

ASEAN's differences with China varied among the members but were real. ASEAN governments opposed Chinese domination of Cambodia, and distrusted what they tended to view as China's overly punitive stance toward Hanoi and Beijing's distinct favoritism toward the Khmer Rouge. Unlike Beijing, ASEAN did not regard Vietnam as a Soviet proxy.

ASEAN's reasons for a firm stance against the Vietnamese occupation focused on the security of Thailand, which was gravely threatened by the loss of the Cambodian "buffer"; the continued disruption of Southeast Asia coming from Hanoi's abetting the massive exodus of Indochinese migrants, and its ambiguous relations with communist insurgents in ASEAN countries; and Hanoi's close ties with Moscow, which acted to exacerbate great power tensions in Southeast Asia.

In the mid-1980s, ASEAN had seen some success in its opposition to the Vietnamese occupation. A case in point was their leadership in the annual lopsided votes in the U.N. General Assembly condemning the Vietnamese occupation. Moreover, ASEAN members' growing importance as key actors in the political discussions over Cambodia's future prompted China, the USSR, the United States and others to seek the approval of the noncommunist Southeast Asian states.

For the United States, too, there appeared to be little reason for change. The United States confined its leadership role to the international refugee and relief effort, where it made a very substantial contribution. In other areas, the United States followed ASEAN's lead. It supported ASEAN's international political campaign and used U.S. international influence to mobilize diplomatic and economic pressures on Vietnam. Washington reiterated its security commitment to Thailand, expedited arms shipments to Bangkok during periods of heavy Vietnamese pressure on the border, and modestly increased its military assistance to the other ASEAN states. Washington did not play a direct military role in the conflict, though in the mid-1980s it began to provide publicly small-scale nonlethal military assistance to noncommunist Cambodian resistance forces.

U.S. support for ASEAN served substantial American interests in the well-being and good will of its members and in the strength of an organization that had become a major factor for East Asian peace and stability and an influential voice in the Third World. ASEAN was one of America's largest trading partners. Three of its members commanded the straits connecting the Pacific and Indian oceans. And the Philippines hosted strategically vital U.S. air and naval bases.

Despite continued U.S. difficulties in coming to terms with the failure of the U.S. involvement in Indochina in 1975, this low-cost and cost-efficient U.S. policy met with little criticism at home. There were some critics who argued that in supporting the ASEAN position and failing to normalize its own relations with Vietnam, the United States was losing significant opportunities to influence Hanoi's policies, loosen its ties with Moscow, and curb Soviet influence in the region. However, policymakers were impressed by the constraints on American leverage imposed by its limited role and the complexities of the Hanoi-Beijing-Moscow relationship. A shift toward accommodation with Hanoi was seen neither to advance prospects for a Cambodian settlement nor reduce Vietnam's incentives for permitting Soviet military access to its ports and airfields. Moreover, accommodation was seen to seriously damage the U.S. relationship with ASEAN and weaken the organization itself.

Elements of Change: The Role of Vietnam

Conventional wisdom has held that Hanoi's ability to defeat both the French and the United States rested heavily on the Vietnamese communists' ability to "outlast" the Western adversaries whose policies were subject to the changing preferences of a democratic electorate. Thus, it is historically ironic that the main catalyst for change in the Cambodian stalemale came from Hanoi itself. To be sure the Vietnamese were subjected to a range of pressures which pushed them to a decision to put aside past talk about the "irreversibility" about the situation in Cambodia, to agree to withdraw their troops, and to begin more meaningful talks on possible political compromises in Cambodia. And, other participants also showed some degree of flexibility from time to time. But the process leading to the more fluid situation we face in Cambodia in the 1990s can trace its origins to changes in Vietnam's calculus in Cambodia in the mid-1980s.

At present, Vietnam is in the midst of the most important policy transition since communist forces succeeded in defeating U.S.-backed noncommunist forces in South Vietnam 15 years ago. Analysts differ as to the precise starting point for the transition, but it appears that a key turning point was reached at the Sixth Vietnamese Party Congress in December 1986. Developments since that time have included the most widespread leadership changes in Hanoi's 35 years of communist rule, domestic political reforms, and major shifts in economic policy and international relations.

Up to the mid-1980s, Western analysts were generally pessimistic about prospects for significant change in Vietnamese policies.[3] Hanoi was expected to continue programs designed to impose the communist system on the economically more advanced and politically more pluralistic south. The Vietnamese economy was expected to remain in a depressed condition, isolated from much of the noncommunist world, and heavily dependent on Soviet bloc economic support. Politically, the "old guard" leaders appeared to dominate most decisions. They had led the communist victories against the French and the Americans, and had sought in 1978 to achieve Vietnamese goals in Cambodia through military invasion and occupation. They were characterized by cohesion and enduring values of single-mindedness, tenacity, the importance of military force as a policy instrument, and placing political, ideological and military goals ahead of economic goals.

Vietnam's foreign policy was dominated by Hanoi's drive to control Laos and Cambodia and by its rivalry with and fear of China. Vietnam needed its close relationship with the Soviet Union to achieve its objectives in Indochina and deal with Chinese and other international opposition to its military occupation of Cambodia. The Soviets, in turn, were willing to provide needed support in return for benefits including access to Vietnamese air and naval bases for Soviet forces. U.S.-Vietnamese relations were at an impasse over Cambodia and little progress was being made on resolving the issue of U.S. missing in action (MIAs) and other humanitarian questions resulting from the Vietnam war.

Events after Vietnam's military invasion of Cambodia in 1978 appeared to reduce the chances of significant change. They set the stage for a prolonged military stalemate and international confrontation. On one side were the Vietnamese client regime in Phnom Penh, the People's Republic of Kampuchea -- PRK, Vietnam and the Soviet Union. On the other side were the Khmer Rouge and two other Cambodian resistance groups, China, Thailand, other Southeast Asian countries, the United States, and other western-aligned countries.

As noted in greater detail in the sections below, Vietnam initiated in 1986 a series of domestic and foreign policy changes. Reform-minded leaders were appointed to senior positions and began economic and foreign policies designed to improve living standards, open more economic opportunities, and ease Vietnam's isolation. They began substantial troop withdrawals from Cambodia; showed greater flexibility over a peace agreement there; and took initiatives on important humanitarian issues, including the U.S. MIAs. The reasons for the new Vietnamese policies involved several domestic and foreign considerations:[4]

- A major generational change involving the top level of Vietnamese party, government and army leaders. Current leaders are less intransigent than the previous generation of "old guards," who led the Vietnamese communists to victory against the French and the United States. They are more sensitive to the fact that their political standing rests to a considerable degree on their ability to improve the livelihood of the Vietnamese people through domestic reforms and international initiatives designed to reduce Vietnam's isolation stemming from its 10 year occupation of Cambodia.

- Continued dismal economic conditions in Vietnam. This has resulted in recurring food shortages; rampant inflation; and isolation from most sources of technology, capital and other assistance as a result of the international restrictions imposed on Vietnam by much of the world community, outside of the Soviet bloc, on account of Vietnam's military occupation of Cambodia. World Bank, International Monetary Fund (IMF), and other western aid has been reduced to a trickle. Trade opportunities are difficult to arrange in the face of international trading restrictions.

- The inability of Vietnam and its client regime in Cambodia, the PRK, to eliminate armed opposition in Cambodia, to reduce foreign support for the armed opposition, or to end the international pressure on Vietnam over the Cambodian occupation. China maintains several hundred thousand troops along Vietnam's northern border and provides arms and other support to the three Cambodian resistance groups. The ASEAN governments back Thailand in providing safe haven for the three Cambodian resistance groups; lead international political efforts to condemn the Vietnamese occupation at the United Nations; and reportedly provide some material support to resistance groups led by Sihanouk and Son Sann. (ASEAN opposes support for the Khmer Rouge even though Thailand provides important safe haven for them and allows Chinese supplies to reach the Khmer Rouge via Thai territory.) The United States follows the lead of ASEAN in pressing Vietnam politically; maintains an economic embargo against Vietnam; and provides modest amounts of nonlethal support to the resistance groups led by Sihanouk and Son Sann. (The United

States, like ASEAN, opposes support for the Khmer Rouge.)
Japan and other western-oriented developed countries also
follow ASEAN's lead in pressing Hanoi politically over
Cambodia.   Their restrictions on economic interaction with
Vietnam vary, though they are generally less restrictive than
the United States.

- A marked change in Moscow's previous full support for the
  Vietnamese occupation of Cambodia. Officials in Moscow used
  to steadfastly defend their "socialist ally" against the opposition
  of China and the West in arguing for the need for the world
  to accept Hanoi's "fait accompli." Soviet officials continue to
  provide material support (valued at about $3 billion a year)
  and to give general public backing to Vietnamese and PRK
  positions. But recently they have strongly focused on the need
  to reach a compromise settlement, have privately complained
  about Vietnamese intransigence, and have noted that Soviet aid
  will be cut back in the near future.

Indeed, behind Moscow's changed approach lies a new emphasis by
Soviet leader Gorbachev to limit Soviet commitments to expensive
clients abroad and to break out of the international isolation caused by
the Brezhnev-era decision to use military power and assistance to
spread Soviet influence in such Third World areas as Afghanistan,
Angola, and Indochina.   In Asia, Gorbachev has been particularly
solicitous of China.   He apparently sees improved Sino-Soviet relations
as an important step in efforts to break out of the Soviet Union's
isolated position, spread its political influence, and increase its
economic opportunities in the region.   Gorbachev has publicly
expressed a willingness to end Soviet access to bases in Vietnam (a
major presumed Soviet interest in Vietnam) in exchange for the U.S.
ending access to bases in the Philippines.   This may indicate that the
USSR no longer sees those bases as critically important in Moscow's
strategy in Asia.

Leadership Changes and Political Reform

The new generation of power holders in Vietnam is more flexible
than past leaders in grappling with economic difficulties, political
malaise, and international isolation. At present, it is probably safe to
say that no one in the Vietnamese leadership stands directly against
the idea of internal economic reform or adjustment in foreign policy.
But less flexible officials, who   worry about diminution of their

political control and other interests, remain strong in slowing or obstructing change.

In a certain sense, the Vietnamese are following the example of Soviet and, at least until 1989, Chinese leaders in reforming their leadership and economy and attempting to ease tensions over foreign affairs. The Vietnamese reforms are relatively recent, however, and the support they enjoy among senior level leaders is decidedly mixed. Most notably, Vietnam's dynamic party General Secretary, Nguyen Van Linh, has been an important force for recent change, thereby serving a role similar to that played by the Soviet Union's Mikhail Gorbachev and China's Deng Xiaoping. But Linh is not in good health and has been expected to retire. His successor will be chosen by a Vietnamese party hierarchy much more representative of less flexible, less reform minded officials than either that of the USSR or until recently, China.[5]

The leadership changes at the landmark Sixth Party Congress in December 1986 saw the three top party leaders--Truong Chinh, 79, party chief and president; Premier Pham Van Dong, 80, and Le Duc Tho, 76, a key party strategist--step down because of "their advanced age and bad health." Chinh and Tho had in fact resisted quitting and agreed to step down only under party pressure a few days before the congress opened, diplomats reported.[6]

Three other members of the politburo--Defense Minister Van Tien Dung, Gen. Chu Huy Man and former vice-premier To Huu--were ousted. Dung and Man had been criticized within the army for their autocratic styles; Huu lost his job as vice-premier after being blamed for a disastrous currency change and resulting runaway inflation in September 1985.

Outgoing party chief Chinh told the congress that the party leadership was responsible for many of the country's problems. "We frankly analyze and bravely admit the serious and longstanding shortcomings and mistakes as concerns major viewpoints and policies, strategic guidance and the organization of work." Responsibility for these shortcomings and mistakes," Chinh said, "rest first of all with the party central committee, the political bureau, the secretariat and with the council of ministers." He called for "bold renovations" to invigorate the country's moribund economy.[7]

Nguyen Van Linh, who is often called a reformer, replaced Chinh as party chief. Linh, a northerner who spent most of his adult life in the south, is credited with encouraging economic decentralization when he served as party secretary in Ho Chi Minh City (formerly called Saigon).

Nevertheless, the continued power of the "old guard" in the leadership was seen when Prime Minister Pham Hung died in March 1988. Linh's choice of Do Muoi over reformer Vo Van Kiet to replace him was seen as a concession by the reformers to the coalition of less reform-minded leaders concerned about diminishing party strength and control. Ironically, the circumstances surrounding Muoi's election highlighted their concern. First, National Assembly members demanded that two candidates be permitted to run, challenging for the first time the central committee's nominee for a key government post. As a result, Muoi, the party's choice was required to face Vo Van Kiet, the nominee of delegates from the south, where Muoi was particularly unpopular because of his key role in introducing repressive socialist policies in the late 1970s. The normal unanimous victory of the party's candidate was compromised. Muoi gained only 64 percent of the assembly's 496 votes. This underlined the concern of less reform minded party leaders that political liberalization posed a threat to party control.[8]

The dissent seen in the National Assembly debate reflected an opening in political debate and discussion on many sensitive issues. A fight initiated by Nguyen Van Linh against massive corruption, for example, encouraged private and official criticism of public policy. The press became an aggressive critic of government policy, although it retained its traditional role as a tool of the party hierarchy and a guardian of party discipline. Acting as vanguard, it was instrumental in the party's removal of the party provincial secretary   Thanh Hoa, whose position was widely regarded as impregnable despite his well publicized abuses of office. By 1988, Linh had succeeded in replacing almost all of the country's 40 province secretaries and 80 percent of the 400 or so district party chiefs. Over one thousand party cadres were tried for corruption in the first six months of the year, and, in an effort to combat future corruption, the central committee, at its fifth plenum in June, 1988, agreed to a new election system in which one third of the central committee membership would be replaced every time an election for top leaders was held.

The prospects for continued political reform were clouded as a result of Hanoi's reaction to the political crackdown in China in mid-1989 and the unprecedented radical political changes in Eastern Europe and the Soviet Union at the turn of the year. The Vietnamese party leaders seemed determined to maintain the party's dominant role and to limit dissent. In March 1990, the Vietnamese party announced at the end of the lengthy central committee meeting that a prominent political reformer was being removed from the politburo and that political reforms would move slowly.

Economic Developments and Reforms

Political infighting affected the regime's ability to deal with pressing economic problems. Party chief Linh's initiatives for dealing with the country's economic problems were bold, as might have been suggested by a statement he made at the beginning of 1988 proposing that Vietnam could learn lessons from the capitalist world. However, by January 1988, a coalition of opposing forces within the party's collective leadership had already effectively denied him the consensus he needed to implement his plans. Consequently, Linh's powers to effect change appeared to wane as the severity of the country's economic crisis deepened. And Linh's declining health and the likelihood of his replacement added to uncertainty over economic policy.

With an economy already crippled by an inflation rate at times approaching 1,000 percent and an unemployment rate reported to be almost 20 percent, Vietnam faced a food crisis in spring 1988 that analysts attributed to mismanagement, corruption, and transportation problems. Ten million Vietnamese in eight northern provinces were affected, forcing Vietnam, a country once self-sufficient in rice, to appeal for 120,000 tons of international food aid. Hanoi officials blamed the crisis on inflated provincial reporting of 1987 rice yields, but claimed a sufficient amount of rice existed within the country to resolve the shortage. The country's primitive transportation network prevented its proper distribution, however. And the low official price of rice offered little incentive for peasants in the more productive south to sell their surplus rice to the government for distribution in the north. The severity of the situation prompted the National Assembly in June 1988 to openly criticize the government's economic performance and to accuse government ministers by name of mishandling the food crisis. Vo Van Kiet, in his capacity as acting premier, assumed full responsibility.

In 1990, Vietnam was able to export sizeable quantities of rice. But an important economic problem for the regime remained the development of an effective strategy to deal with food production and high inflation. Since 1975 the regime had zig-zagged through various economic changes, initially toward centralization, collectivization, eradication of private enterprise and radical socialist transformation. In the mid-1970s there was a precipitous campaign to dismantle the south's free enterprise economic infrastructure and integrate it with the north's centralized system. The results were disastrous, and the move further alienated the nation's most productive agricultural region. After 1978, the government oscillated between tentative economic liberalization and tighter controls, and deterioration continued. Driven by food shortages and plummeting productivity generally, in June 1985 the party announced and began to implement "drastic and extraordinary reforms" aimed at reducing bureaucratic centralism and stimulating local management and decision-making authority on prices, wages and production schedules.[9]

The regime's most egregious error was the currency devaluation in September 1985. Overnight ten dong were devalued to one and the maximum permissible family cash holding was limited to 2,000 dong (about U.S. $20.00). Families with more than 2,000 dong cash lost their savings. The government attempted, unsuccessfully, to keep the plan secret. Panic, catastrophic losses and massive illegal investments and hoarding followed. Vietnam continues to suffer the consequences of the inflation hike that took off after this event.

The economy was the major focus of the Sixth Communist Party Congress in December 1986. Remedial measures implementing the decisions taken then are still flowing today from Hanoi. Yet, government and party officials openly admit that the economic plight remains serious.

In the wake of the Congress, Vietnam's economy is a mixed bag of internal contradictions and confusing administrative guidelines. Cynicism and disregard of regulations are the rule; a gray market has emerged as the real economy in many sectors, and there are multiple dollar exchange rates. For a time, inflation was running between 500 to 1,000 percent annually for staple commodities, and people living on fixed incomes were especially hurt. Even with subsidized food rations, civil servants must take on second and third jobs to survive, with adverse effects on an already sluggish bureaucracy. Probably the largest single source of hard currency for Vietnam is remittances by overseas Vietnamese who support their relatives by sending cash or marketable goods. The annual total of several hundred million dollars contributes importantly to the south's appearance of wealth. The government encourages this cash inflow.

Unemployed persons and homeless families are common in the main cities. There is a desperate shortage of housing nation-wide. Government officials at every level admit bluntly that the standard of living for the great majority of Vietnamese today is lower than at any time since 1975.

To change the situation, government officials are carrying out various internal economic reforms and are trying to open the Vietnamese economy to foreign investments, technology, and financial assistance from noncommunist countries. Some progress has been made, but the latter effort remains hampered by several factors including Vietnam's international isolation caused by its military occupation of Cambodia.

In the late 1980s, the government introduced regulations that attempted to increase the farmer's incentive to produce higher yields by turning over more responsibility for the rice growing process to the individual. Land tenure laws were modified to guarantee farmers a 10-year tenure on the land, and the contract system between peasants and the government was revised to permit peasants to keep 45-50 percent of their output, a substantial increase over the 25 percent formerly allowed. Other reforms removed restrictions on private-production enterprises in Hanoi, introduced the concept of developing industry outside the state-run sector, and granted the south autonomy to undertake economic policies separate from those adopted nationally. A program was also implemented to stabilize the economy and control inflation by limiting government spending and state subsidies, liberalizing wage and price controls, promoting efficiency, and rationalizing the country's foreign exchange rate. As an economizing measure, a plan was introduced to cut the country's armed forces to "around one percent" of the population, a cut that would mean halving the 1.26 million man army to between 600,000 and 700,000. (At present, Vietnam has the fifth largest armed forces in the world.) Such a cut, according to the plan, was expected to free both funds and manpower for transfer to the economic sector.[10]

Developments in foreign economic relations included a January 1988 revised foreign investment code to attract more foreign investors. The code offered a two-year tax moratorium for joint ventures, tax exemptions for certain imports and exports, and guarantees that investment capital would not be expropriated or joint ventures nationalized. It was also expected to provide preferential treatment for overseas Vietnamese. Day-to-day operations of enterprises, nevertheless, remained under the central bureaucracy's control in the guise of a new body called the State Organ for Management of Foreign Investment.

Uncontrolled inflation, uncertainty over how Vietnam intended to implement its investment code, and widespread opposition to Vietnam's military occupation in Cambodia continued to discourage foreign companies. But the number of visiting foreign businessmen grew and trade with established trading partners -- such as Japan, Singapore, Hong Kong, France, Indonesia, and India -- increased. Thailand signed a joint venture agreement, and the French-owned Atatel Company contracted to equip the country with a new telephone network. Oil exploration contracts were signed with the Indian Oil and Natural Gas Commission, Belgium's Petrofina, and Shell Oil of the Netherlands, but most of the estimated 150,000 to 280,000 tons of oil to be produced in 1988 was expected to come from Soviet-Vietnamese joint ventures.

Foreign Policy Changes: Movement on Cambodia[11]

Few analysts judge that Vietnam has abandoned its longstanding effort to seek control of Indochina. Vietnamese leaders are still believed to seek indigenous governments in Cambodia and Laos that respond to Hanoi's political direction, are closely tied to and dependent on Vietnam through trade, investment, and military ties, and do not harbor groups that are unfriendly to Hanoi. While Hanoi has achieved this goal in Laos, its efforts in Cambodia have not been successful.

Vietnam has moved substantially from its previous seemingly intransigent position that the situation in Cambodia was "irreversible." Hanoi and its Cambodian client regime, the PRK, no longer require preconditions involving the "removal of outside threats" (presumably referring to Chinese pressure in particular) and removal of the Khmer Rouge. Indeed, the Vietnamese and the PRK have taken part in talks with the Khmer Rouge as well as with the other two Cambodian resistance groups. They also have indicated that they do not oppose a "political" role for the Khmer Rouge in a future Cambodian government, although they strongly demand the dismantling of Khmer Rouge armed forces. Most importantly, Vietnam withdrew 50,000 troops from Cambodia in 1988, reducing its troop strength to about 70,000; and it said it completed its withdrawal in 1989.

In this new situation, Vietnam has engaged in maneuvering over a political agreement in Cambodia. It also has attempted to improve its relations with China, ASEAN and the United States and to get them to curb support for the Cambodian resistance as Vietnamese forces withdrew. Hanoi has focused attention on the Khmer Rouge forces, the most capable of the three resistance groups, which receive support from China.

In response to this Vietnamese effort, as well as to increasing, unfavorable international attention to longstanding Chinese support for the Khmer Rouge, China began to adjust its position on a possible peace agreement. By early 1989, Chinese leaders said they would support a gradual cut off of supplies to the resistance following a Vietnamese withdrawal, provided Hanoi would cut off its support for the PRK.

Beijing showed little interest in responding positively to Hanoi's repeated calls for talks to deal with bilateral problems until early 1989 when it was reported that talks at the vice foreign minister level had begun. Military tension along the border remained at a low level with the notable exception of a clash in March 1988 between Sino-Vietnamese warships over disputed Spratly Islands in the South China Sea.

Vietnam's troop withdrawal from Cambodia and more flexible stance on a peace agreement in Cambodia substantially improved Vietnamese relations with ASEAN. ASEAN remains unified in backing the Cambodian resistance's demand for a complete, verified, and unconditional Vietnamese withdrawal. But the ASEAN countries also have been very active in developing common ground between Hanoi and the PRK on one side, and the Cambodian resistance and its international backers on the other, in order to achieve a peace agreement that would provide for a Vietnamese troop withdrawal but preclude the return of the genocidal practices of the Khmer Rouge. Meanwhile, in response to a rise in the outflow of Vietnamese migrants generated by Vietnamese economic difficulties and other conditions, Hanoi assured its neighbors that it would ease their burdens as countries of first asylum by reversing a policy that forbids the return of such migrants to Vietnam. Hanoi also proposed to open discussion with Southeast Asian officials on ending the exodus, and participated in an international meetings on Indochinese migrants in 1989 and 1990.

The Vietnamese military withdrawal from Cambodia and increased flexibility on a peace agreement also substantially improved the atmosphere in relations with the United States. Moreover, Hanoi has recently shown increased flexibility in dealing with the MIA and other humanitarian issues in U.S.-Vietnamese relations. At the end of 1988, it returned several dozen sets of remains said to be those of U.S. military personnel; began a series of joint survey excavations of sites where U.S. aircraft were known to have crashed during the Vietnam War; and took other steps that encouraged some U.S. policymakers to be more optimistic about progress in resolving such longstanding humanitarian issues. Other Americans were more circumspect.

Notes

1.　See, for example, U.S. Congress, Senate Foreign Relations Committee, *Vietnam's Future Policies and Role in Southeast Asia* (Washington, DC: U.S. GPO, 1982); Dick Clark and David Carpenter, *The Third Indochina War: Prospects for Peace* (Washington, DC: Aspen Institute for Humanistic Studies, 1987); and Evelyn Colbert, "Standing Pat," *Foreign Policy* (Spring 1984): pp. 139-155.

2.　For background on these issues, see the competing perspectives in Nayan Chanda, *Brother Enemy* (NY: Harcourt, Brace, Jovanovich, 1986); and Robert Ross, *The Indochina Tangle* (NY: Columbia University Press, 1988).

3.　See sources listed in note 1.

4.   For general discussion of these developments, see *The Far Eastern Economic Review, Asia Yearbook,* for relevant years; and the annual survey of Vietnam that appears each January in *Asian Survey.* See also the regularly updated "Vietnam-U.S. Relations" (CRS Issue Brief 87210); the regularly updated "Cambodian Crisis: Problems of a Settlement and Policy Dilemmas for the United States" (CRS Issue Brief 89020); and Robert Goldich regularly updated, "POWs and MIAs in Indochina and Korea" (CRS Issue Brief 88061).

5.   According to some analysts, despite the strong presence of less reform-minded officials, the party hierarchy is also collectively intent on preserving the current balance of "conservatives" and "reformers." Thus, if Nguyen Van Linh does retire, there is speculation that a conservative, perhaps Do Muoi, will also be required to step down for the sake of balance.   (From an interview with U.S. Government Official, Washington, DC: February 1989.)

6.   This discussion of personnel changes and the 1986 Party Congress is based on *The Far Eastern Economic Review, Asia 1988 Yearbook,* pp. 252-253. Tho reportedly still wields considerable power through his proteges, many of whom owe their positions on the political bureau and the central committee to him.

7.   See note 6.

8.   This and the following paragraphs are based on Ronald Cima, "Vietnam in 1988," *Asian Survey* (January 1989): pp. 88-96.

9.   This and the following four paragraphs are based on Frederick Z. Brown, "The Next War in Vietnam," *The International Economy* (Nov.-Dec. 1988): pp. 47, 49.

10. This and the following two paragraphs are based on Ronald Cima, "Vietnam in 1988."

11. For background see "Cambodian Crisis"   (CRS Issue Brief 89020).

4

U.S. Policy Concerns in Cambodia and Vietnam

Vietnam's military withdrawal from Cambodia, efforts to reach a negotiated agreement to the Cambodian conflict, and more forthcoming stance on some humanitarian issues of importance to the United States increased the debate in the United States over the appropriate U.S. policy toward the Cambodian crisis and over the related question of U.S. normalization of relations with Vietnam.[1]

In particular, the Vietnamese withdrawal prompted U.S. decision-makers to reassess the past low-level U.S. association with the Cambodian resistance, with a view toward insuring that the Khmer Rouge, the most powerful resistance group, would be held in check in the newly fluid situation in Cambodia. Some U.S. officials favored a policy that would give greater support to the two noncommunist resistance groups, led respectively by Prince Sihanouk and Son Sann. But other officials, especially in Congress, judged that these groups were too weak or otherwise ineffective in blocking the Khmer Rouge. Several members of Congress judged that in order to check Khmer Rouge power, the United States should move to break its diplomatic and economic embargo against the communist PRK government in Phnom Penh and its Vietnamese backers in Hanoi. Only they were seen to have sufficient power to deal with Pol Pot and his associates. Arguments in favor of this approach were strengthened by Hanoi's concurrent flexibility on the return of the remains of U.S. MIAs, the emigration of Vietnamese who were closely associated with the United States, and other issues. Nevertheless, strong opposition to improved relations with Phnom Penh and Hanoi continued to be registered by U.S. policymakers in the administration and Congress who were loath to legitimize Hanoi's invasion of Cambodia in 1978, to accommodate Vietnam's obvious desire for normal U.S.-Vietnamese relations until Hanoi met firm U.S. preconditions, or to recognize a Cambodian government headed by officials who had been part of the Khmer Rouge during its genocidal reign.

U.S. leaders also focused on various efforts by third parties to reach a settlement in Cambodia. Efforts by ASEAN countries, France, Australia, and the United Nations were prominently considered in the late 1980s and in 1990. U.S. officials actively sought to monitor, and participate when appropriate, in these efforts in order to insure U.S. interests would be safeguarded in any possible settlement. U.S. support was actively sought by various proponents of peace plans. In the new situation in Cambodia, U.S. leverage was seen as more important than in the past. This leverage stemmed from several factors:

- The United States was one of five members of the U.N. Security Council and a key financial backer of U.N. operations, including possible U.N. peacekeeping operations as part of a Cambodian settlement.

- U.S. covert and overt aid to the noncommunist Cambodian resistance was a key element in the international support received by those two groups.

- Ending the U.S. diplomatic and economic embargo against Vietnam was seen to be of profound importance to Hanoi leaders in their efforts to break out of their diplomatic-economic isolation that had resulted from their invasion of Cambodia. It was seen to be the main incentive that could be offered by the United States in order to encourage Hanoi to press its client regime in Phnom Penh to be flexible over a future Cambodian settlement.

- The United States exerted influence on the lending policies of the international financial institutions and had some influence on the lending policies followed by other possible sources of economic assistance to Indochina, notably Japan.

- The United States remained an ally of Thailand, the key ASEAN conduit of support for all three Cambodian resistance groups and base for the 300,000 displaced Cambodians who provided the new recruits for the resistance.

- Despite the downturn in U.S.-Chinese relations following Beijing's hard crackdown on dissent in mid-1989, the United States sustained limited high-level communications and possibly considerable influence with China, the main backer of the Khmer Rouge resistance focus.

- Radical change in Eastern Europe and internal instability in the Soviet Union reinforced Soviet President Gorbachev's need for greater outreach to the West. This appeared to give the interests of the United States greater importance in Soviet calculations of policies in areas of past controversy in U.S.-Soviet relations. In particular, it seemed to promise a Soviet approach toward a settlement in Cambodia more in accord with U.S. interests.

This chapter reviews recent efforts to reach a Cambodian peace agreement, assesses the positions and interests of the contending parties, and examines U.S. policy dilemmas and possible options. Because U.S. policy toward the Cambodian problem is closely related to the state of U.S.-Vietnamese relations, the chapter concludes with an examination of U.S.-Vietnamese relations: it reviews developments since 1975 and assess competing U.S. policy approaches.

Cambodia: Efforts to Reach a Peace Accord

Highlights of the various developments in discussions on a possible peace agreement or ceasefire in Cambodia included the following:

- In December 1987, PRK Prime Minister Hun Sen and resistance leader Prince Sihanouk held three days of talks in Paris.

- In May 1988, the Vietnamese announced what they said would be the withdrawal of 50,000 troops from Cambodia by the end of the year.

- In July 1988, four days of talks involving the PRK and the three Cambodian resistance groups were held in Indonesia. The so-called Jakarta Informal Meeting or "JIM" talks also involved direct participation by Vietnam, Laos, and ASEAN. A round of talks was held in November 1988 in Paris among the PRK and two of the three Cambodian resistance groups (the Khmer Rouge did not attend). A second round of "JIM" talks ended inconclusively in February 1989. A series of talks among Prince Sihanouk, Son Sann, and the PRK's Hun Sen were held in Indonesia in early May 1989. Sihanouk met with Hun Sen in Paris in July 1989.

- An international conference on Cambodia began in Paris July 30, 1989, and was suspended a month later. It was attended by

18 nations, two international organizations, and the four contending Cambodian factions. (U.S. Secretary of State James Baker attended the opening sessions.) On August 1, the conference adopted a general blueprint for peace, broke into smaller groups to study issues, and agreed to fund a U.N. fact-finding mission to Cambodia in August. The conference failed to bridge differences over key issues such as the role of international supervision of Vietnam's withdrawal and peace in Cambodia, and the future makeup of the government of Cambodia.

•   The five permanent members of the U.N. Security Council met in Paris in January 1990 in the first of a series of meetings to discuss a possible expanded U.N. peacekeeping and monitoring role in Cambodia under terms of a peace proposal championed by the Australian government.

•   Another round of talks in Jakarta among the Cambodian opponents ended in failure on March 1, 1990.

•   A round of talks in Tokyo among the Cambodian opponents ended inconclusively in June 1990.

•   U.S. officials began talks on peace in Cambodia with Vietnamese officials in New York on August 6, 1990. This represented an initiative by the Bush administration.

•   The four Cambodian factions met in Indonesia in September 1990 to endorse a detailed peace plan approved in August by the five permanent U.N. Security Council members. Concurrently, the United States began official contacts with the Phnom Penh government.

Positions of the Contending Parties
and Issues in Dispute

The array of local, regional, and international actors with a strong interest in a possible Cambodian peace agreement can be divided into two groups. On one side stand the Vietnamese, with their client regime in Cambodia, the PRK (known since 1989 as the "State of Cambodia"), and backed by the Soviet Union. (Analysts have seen significant divergence over key issues between Hanoi and Phnom Penh, on the one hand, and the Soviet Union on the other. Soviet efforts in the late 1980s to promote a compromise settlement and to improve their relations with China, ASEAN, and the West appeared to widen this perceived gap.)

Opposed to this group is the often highly factionalized coalition of the three Cambodian resistance groups (i.e., those led respectively by the Khmer Rouge, Prince Sihanouk, and Son Sann). The main split in the resistance is between the Khmer Rouge, backed mainly by China, and the two noncommunist forces, led by Prince Sihanouk and Son Sann, backed mainly by ASEAN and the United States. The coalition and their international backers were unified in their desire to rid Cambodia of the Vietnamese military occupation. But they are seen to differ strongly over other questions like the future role of the Khmer Rouge in Cambodia and the extent to which Vietnam should be allowed to exert influence in Cambodian affairs.

Despite the differences and signs of maneuvering within the ranks of each side, however, both sides have come up with general guidelines for a peace agreement. The gaps between these two general positions represent obstacles to a peace agreement. They center in these areas:

1. The Vietnamese-PRK side had insisted that the withdrawal of Vietnamese troops from Cambodia must be linked with the cutoff of outside support for the Cambodian resistance groups. The resistance and their foreign backers at first refused. Chinese officials said that such a cutoff could take place as the Vietnamese withdraw, but it would require a cutoff of Vietnamese support to the PRK as well.

2. The two sides have continued to disagree on the establishment of a future administration in Cambodia. In particular:

    a. Role of PRK: Hanoi and Phnom Penh had wanted the PRK to remain in power until elections for a new government were held; the resistance and their backers had called for the dismantling of the PRK and the establishment of an interim quadripartite coalition government, made up of representatives from the three resistance groups and the PRK, prior to holding elections. In their communique of June 5, 1990, Sihanouk and Hun Sen endorsed the establishment of a "Supreme National Council" in Cambodia until elections could be held. The importance of this step was unclear since the Khmer Rouge refused to endorse the communique.

   b.   Role of Khmer Rouge Forces: Hanoi and Phnom Penh
        have said Khmer Rouge military forces must be
        disbanded. The Cambodian resistance groups, with the
        strong support of China, had held that the Khmer
        Rouge, including a scaled-down version of its army,
        should be a full participant in the quadripartite
        coalition government that would supervise elections
        for a new Cambodian government.   (Sihanouk
        reiterated on June 5, 1990 that the Khmer Rouge
        should be represented in the proposed "Supreme
        National Council.")

   c.   Role of International Supervision: Hanoi and Phnom
        Penh have wanted to place conditions on any
        international supervisory body that would observe
        elections or keep the peace in Cambodia. By contrast,
        the resistance and their backers have called for strong
        international supervision, including armed
        peacekeeping forces.

3.   During the Paris conference in July-August 1989 and again
     during the Jakarta meeting of February-March 1990, the
     Vietnamese-PRK side emphasized the need to condemn past
     Khmer Rouge "genocide" in Cambodia. The resistance forces
     and China in turn emphasized the importance of the
     withdrawal of tens of thousands of Vietnamese troops they
     claimed were "hidden" in PRK army ranks. (See Appendix D
     for a chart listing the two contending groups and their
     differing stances on a peace agreement.)

Competing Interests

The gaps between the two sides' positions on a peace agreement
will be hard to bridge because of each side's competing interests in
Cambodia and because each side will try to protect these interests as
the Cambodian conflict moves into a stage of more extensive
negotiations.

Vietnam, the PRK, and the USSR

Vietnam, the PRK, and the USSR have moved from their previous
seemingly intransigent position that the situation in Cambodia was
"irreversible." Hanoi and the PRK no longer require preconditions
involving the "removal of outside threats" (presumably referring to

Chinese pressure in particular) and removal of the Khmer Rouge. Indeed, in the "JIM" talks, the Vietnamese and the PRK have taken part in talks with the Khmer Rouge as well as with the other two Cambodian resistance groups. They also have indicated at times that they do not oppose a "political" role for the Khmer Rouge in a future Cambodian government, although they strongly demand the dismantling of Khmer Rouge armed forces.

The new Vietnamese flexibility is due to the costs of Vietnam's prolonged military occupation and changed international circumstances. These have prompted the Vietnamese and their Phnom Penh clients to seek a compromise political solution to what had been viewed heretofore as a largely military problem.

Vietnam's calculus (and that of its client, the PRK) involves several considerations including:

- the inability of Vietnamese and PRK forces to eliminate armed opposition in Cambodia or reduce foreign support for it.

- the cost of the protracted international isolation of Vietnam brought on by the Vietnamese military occupation of Cambodia. World Bank, IMF, and other western aid has been reduced to a minimum, and trade opportunities are difficult to arrange in the face of a U.S.-backed trading embargo.

- a marked change in Soviet attitudes towards the conflict in Cambodia. Vietnamese officials have publicly raised the possibility that the USSR would sacrifice its interests in Vietnam for the sake of an accommodation with China.

As noted earlier, Soviet officials used to steadfastly defend their "socialist ally" against the opposition of China and the West in arguing for the need for the world to accept Hanoi's "fait accompli." Soviet officials continue to provide material support (over $3 billion a year in economic and military aid) and to give general public backing to Vietnamese and PRK positions. In 1989, they reportedly gave Phnom Penh double the amount of military equipment delivered in 1988. But aid levels are expected to drop quickly and the assistance Vietnam and Cambodia previously received from Eastern Europe is also falling rapidly. The Soviets also have strongly focused on the need to reach a compromise settlement, and privately they sometimes complain about Vietnamese intransigence. Soviet air forces based in Vietnam were cut back sharply in late 1989.[2]

Cambodian Resistance and Its International Supporters

Analysts often marvel that the three resistance groups and their respective leaders have been able to maintain any semblance of a unified stance as the so-called Coalition Government of Democratic Kampuchea. The leaders have deep historical grudges against one another, and their forces are reported to spend a good deal of effort defending themselves against depredations of other factions rather than fighting the Vietnamese or the PRK forces. As noted earlier, the main split in the resistance is between the Khmer Rouge, backed mainly by China, and the noncommunist forces, backed mainly by ASEAN and the United States. The Khmer Rouge has a legacy of genocidal policies practiced when it wielded power in Cambodia in 1975-79; it continues to impose draconian control measures among the people under its current supervision; and it is by far the strongest military and political organization among the three factions. As a result, the Khmer Rouge is greatly feared by the other two factions, who along with their international backers are concerned with driving out the Vietnamese, but are also concerned with keeping the Khmer Rouge from gaining predominant power once again.

The three coalition partners are obviously interested in maximizing their chances to gain and hold power in a possible future Cambodian government as the Vietnamese withdraw. They are reported to differ on a number of issues involving the future role of the Khmer Rouge and PRK forces. Prince Sihanouk's and Son Sann's followers are seen as looking for ways to curb the Khmer Rouge's power now that most if not all of the Vietnamese forces have left. This includes the possibility of working more closely with the PRK forces in a cooperative effort to restrict the Khmer Rouge's influence. The Khmer Rouge also sees the possibility of an alignment of forces against it in a post-Vietnamese withdrawal situation. It is resupplying and deploying its forces and taking other steps to build its ability to influence events in Cambodia. The Khmer Rouge forces reportedly made battlefield gains and also improved their political influence in the Cambodian countryside during 1990.

The Asian backers of the resistance agree on the need to work together to assure the Vietnamese military withdrawal, but they differ on the degree of influence the Khmer Rouge, Vietnam, and the PRK should have in the post-withdrawal Cambodia. China supports the Khmer Rouge's role in a settlement and warns of Vietnam's alleged intention to beef up the PRK in order to control the situation in Cambodia following the Vietnamese troop withdrawal. In ASEAN, opinion covers a broad range. For example, there are some officials in Thailand who have reportedly built a working relationship with the

Khmer Rouge and see them as providing a useful buffer against what is seen as a likely continued Vietnamese dominance through the PRK of the eastern part of Cambodia; other officials in Thailand are reportedly ready to normalize relations with the PRK to benefit from perceived commercial opportunities in Thai-Cambodian relations; and there are observers in Indonesia who see the Khmer Rouge as a stalking horse for the spread of Chinese influence in Cambodia. They support continued Vietnamese influence there as a buffer to the spread of Chinese influence in the region.

Dilemmas for U.S. Policy

In this evolving situation, U.S. policymakers in Congress and the executive branch face continuing dilemmas for U.S. policy in Cambodia.

On the one hand, the United States has wanted to help check and push back Soviet-backed Vietnamese expansion in Indochina, in the process supporting the position of its treaty ally, Thailand, and the other members of ASEAN. (Strategically-and economically-important communication routes converge in the region, and U.S. investment in and trade with ASEAN has grown rapidly in recent years). Our interest in working with these nations to check Soviet-backed Vietnamese expansion has proceeded in parallel with our cooperation with other Asian regional actors concerned with Soviet and Vietnamese influence, notably China and Japan.

On the other hand, the United States strongly opposes the Khmer Rouge; has been reluctant to get more actively involved in Indochina following the U.S. withdrawal in 1975; and finds that the impasse with Vietnam over Cambodia complicates efforts by those in the United States who wish to improve relations with Vietnam in order to make greater progress in resolving the issue of U.S. servicemen missing in action (MIAs) in Indochina and other humanitarian issues in U.S.-Vietnam relations, or for other reasons. The dilemmas for U.S. policy are sharpened because of the differences among China and ASEAN countries regarding the appropriate role of the Khmer Rouge and Vietnamese influence in Cambodia after the Vietnamese military withdrawal.

Reflecting these conflicting pressures, the United States until recently tried to avoid a high public profile in Cambodia and preferred a policy which followed the lead of the ASEAN states. The United States continued to exert diplomatic pressure and economic sanctions against Vietnam, criticized Soviet support for the Vietnamese occupation, and backed the resistance forces' coalition government in the annual Cambodian Resolution in the United Nations. The United States has contributed to international efforts, mainly through U.N.

organizations and the International Red Cross, to feed the estimated 300,000 displaced Cambodians who reside along the Thai-Cambodian border and make up a popular base for the resistance forces. Such aid was estimated at $15 million annually in the mid-1980s.

Since 1985, the United States has publicly authorized and approved over $3 million annually in nonlethal assistance for the two noncommunist resistance groups. For FY1989, the amount was $5 million. The Administration requested $7 million for FY1990, an amount approved by the House and Senate in separate bills in mid-1989; and it asked for $7 million in aid for FY1991. The United States reportedly has given these same groups larger amounts of covert nonlethal aid over the same period.

Recent Developments and Current Policy Proposals

Over the past few years, the administration and Congress have inserted the United States more prominently into discussions over a Cambodian settlement. In general, U.S. policy has striven to get the Vietnamese to withdraw, to prevent the return of the Khmer Rouge, and to allow the Cambodians to determine their own political future. However, U.S. officials and other Americans disagree on how much and what kind of role the United States can or should play in reaching these goals. Proposals have been laid out that call among other things for strong opposition to the return of the Khmer Rouge; provision of U.S. lethal aid for the noncommunist Cambodian resistance; cutting off U.S. aid to the noncommunist resistance; opening official U.S. contacts with the PRK; and establishment of more U.S. contact with Vietnam. They are treated below. (Proposals concerning the issue of whether the United States should break its diplomatic and economic embargo on Vietnam in the interests of facilitating a Cambodian settlement and for other U.S. policy concerns are considered in a separate section of this chapter, below.)

The proposals address a number of questions and policy dilemmas seen in the U.S. approach to Cambodian related issues at the present time. Such questions include: How can U.S. policy--on the one hand --assist in efforts to pressure the Vietnamese to withdraw from Cambodia, while--on the other hand--avoid the creation of a power vacuum that could be filled by the Khmer Rouge? Is it desirable for U.S. policy to support Sihanouk's call for a four-party interim government, when the two strongest factions in that government would represent the Khmer Rouge and the pro-Vietnamese communist PRK? What is the proper mix of U.S. "carrots" and "sticks" to get the Vietnamese to withdraw from Cambodia and to assist in reaching a peaceful settlement of the conflict?

- **Strong opposition to the return of the Khmer Rouge.**
  H.J.Res. 602 (P.L. 100-502), signed into law in October 1988,
  calls on the United States to take all appropriate measures to
  prevent a return to power of the Khmer Rouge. Specific
  measures include pressing for a cut-off in supplies to the
  Khmer Rouge forces, denying them safe haven, and opening
  Khmer Rouge-controlled refugee camps to international
  inspection and allowing their residents to move freely. These
  measures enjoy strong support in the United States. But they
  could be difficult to implement; and if carried out, they could
  pose difficulties in U.S. relations with those important Asian
  countries, China and Thailand, that have provided the supplies
  and safe haven for the Khmer Rouge over the past decade. As
  noted above, China and Thailand may be less willing to place
  such tight restrictions on the Khmer Rouge. Both China and
  Thailand have adjusted their positions in the face of recent
  strong international opposition to a return to power of the
  Khmer Rouge, although China's sensitivity to such
  international criticism may have been affected by Beijing's
  preoccupation with internal affairs following the brutal June
  1989 crackdown on political dissent in China.

- **Stronger U.S. support for the noncommunist
  Cambodian resistance forces.** Press reports at the time of
  President Reagan's October 1988 meeting with Prince
  Sihanouk (see Chronology, below) indicated that the
  administration planned a significant increase in U.S. overt and
  alleged covert assistance to the two noncommunist resistance
  groups. The Bush administration was reported in April 1989
  to be considering the supply of lethal aid, i.e. weapons, to the
  noncommunist resistance. Congressional supporters for such
  a policy said it would assist those forces' ability to oppose the
  Vietnamese occupiers; and it would strengthen their position
  for future political and military interaction with both the
  Khmer Rouge and the Vietnamese-backed PRK. Opponents
  said it would divide the Cambodian opposition to the Khmer
  Rouge; complicate efforts to get China, the USSR, Vietnam,
  and others to limit their supplies to clients in Cambodia; and
  make the search for a peace settlement in Cambodia more
  complicated.

In April 1989, Senator Pell introduced a resolution to bar U.S.
aid to the noncommunist resistance until it broke formally
with the Khmer Rouge. The measure was opposed by the

administration, the ASEAN governments, and some in Congress.

The administration in late May 1989 reportedly decided to begin giving covert lethal aid to the noncommunist Cambodian resistance. But this approach was strongly criticized by some in Congress as precluding public debate on this important step. In a speech on June 22, 1989, Vice President Quayle called on Congress to debate the issue in considering the Cambodian provision of the annual foreign assistance authorization legislation.

The House passed its version of the foreign assistance authorization bill (H.R. 2655) on June 29, 1989. The bill authorized the aid sought by the administration. The Senate went on record authorizing lethal, as well as nonlethal, aid to the noncommunist resistance in a vote on July 20, 1989, to the State Department authorization bill (S. 1160). While neither bill became law in 1989, the votes could have been seen to provide sufficient sanction for the administration to approach the intelligence committees for approval of covert lethal aid to the noncommunist resistance. Senator Boren, Chairman of the Senate Intelligence Committee, had said in a statement on June 15, 1989, that decisions on issues such as lethal aid to the noncommunist resistance should be decided by Congress openly, not by the intelligence committees alone. Press reports in November 1989 said a secret appendix in the FY1990 defense appropriations bill (H.R. 3072) prevented the administration from using CIA contingency funds for lethal aid to the Cambodian resistance unless the administration first received congressional approval.

• **Cut off U.S. support for the noncommunist resistance.** Congressional actions in 1990 threatened to cut off U.S. financial support for the noncommunist resistance. At issue was the noncommunist resistance's continued battlefield and other reported cooperation with the Khmer Rouge against the PRK -- cooperation that had occurred off-and-on in the past but which was now seen by many in Congress as adverse to the U.S. interest of preventing the growth in power of the Khmer Rouge. Debate over a House foreign aid appropriations bill (H.R. 5114) on June 27, 1990, saw 163 Members vote against $7 million in overt aid to the noncommunist resistance for FY1991 and 260 Members vote in favor. The Senate

Intelligence Committee, reportedly concerned with the noncommunist resistance forces' cooperation with the Khmer Rouge, voted in June 1990 to cut off U.S. covert funding for the noncommunist resistance.

- **Open contacts with the PRK** -- "dear colleague" letters signed by many senators in July 1990 called on the United States to improve contacts with the PRK administration along with initiatives to support international efforts focused on preventing the return to power of the Khmer Rouge. The Bush administration began such contacts in September 1990.

- **Work with Vietnam** -- The administration announced on July 18, 1990, that it would seek contacts with Hanoi to reach a settlement in Cambodia and would no longer support the three party coalition government, including the Khmer Rouge, in the United Nations. In recent years, some members of Congress have called upon the United States to establish offices in Vietnam or to take other steps to facilitate exchanges over MIA and other humanitarian or other issues. Such U.S. flexibility is also said by some to represent a useful way to encourage greater Vietnamese flexibility on Cambodia, and thereby to facilitate Hanoi's military withdrawal and the establishment of peace. But others maintain that any such U.S. initiatives must await complete Vietnamese withdrawal and a peace settlement in Cambodia. To do otherwise, in their view, would only encourage Hanoi to attempt to "hang on" in Cambodia in the face of "vacillating" international opposition. (See separate discussion of this issue in this chapter, below).

- **U.N. role** -- In 1989 and 1990, several members of Congress voiced strong support for U.N.-sponsored negotiations to reach a peace agreement on the basis of a U.N. role in managing the situation in Cambodia until a free and fair election would determine the new Cambodian government. Congressional and broader U.S. interest in this approach rose following the August 1990 agreement on a Cambodian peace plan by the five permanent members of the U.N. Security Council and the general endorsement of that plan by the Cambodian parties in September 1990.

- **Aid to Cambodian children** -- The FY1990 supplemental appropriations bill (H.R. 4404, P.L. 101-302) called for the provision of up to $5 million through international relief agencies to children within Cambodia.

Possible U.S.-Vietnamese Normalization

The Vietnamese troop withdrawal from Cambodia coincided with a more forthcoming Vietnamese stance on various humanitarian issues of importance to the United States. These developments revived discussion among U.S. policymakers between opposing groups who have generally similar goals vis-a-vis-Indochina but who differ on the appropriate U.S. policy toward Vietnam that would help reach those goals. Specifically in regard to reaching a settlement in Cambodia, one group argues that U.S. interest in restoring peace and stability requires continued firm pressure on Vietnam, including continuation of U.S. diplomatic and economic isolation. An opposing group says that success in reaching these goals requires greater U.S. flexibility and accommodation toward Vietnam.

U.S.-Vietnam Relations Since 1975

U.S.-Vietnam diplomatic and economic relations have remained essentially frozen for over a decade. After the communist victory in South Vietnam in April 1975, the United States ended diplomatic relations with Saigon and subjected all economic relations with South Vietnam to the same restrictions that already applied to North Vietnam. These restrictions consisted principally of a virtually total embargo on all commercial and financial transactions with Vietnam, a blocking of all Vietnamese assets in the United States, and a ban on U.S. exports to Vietnam.

The Hanoi government called for talks with the United States on establishing diplomatic relations and demanded that the United States fulfill the provisions of the January 1973 Paris Peace Agreement, including a provision that pledged U.S. post-war aid for Vietnam's reconstruction. The Ford administration rejected Vietnam's demand for aid on grounds that Hanoi had massively violated the Paris Peace Agreement in launching its final military assault against South Vietnam. It also said that there could be no normalization of relations without a full accounting of Americans missing-in-action (MIA) during the war and until Vietnam's longer range intentions in Southeast Asia became more clear. The United States vetoed Vietnam's application for membership in the United Nations on three occasions during 1975-1976.

Policy Initiatives During the Carter Administration

The Carter administration took several steps to improve relations with Vietnam in 1977, but these efforts were progressively frustrated by growing evidence in 1978 that the Vietnamese government was deliberately expelling hundreds of thousands of its citizens and was making military preparations to invade Cambodia. (See Appendix B for a full discussion of the steps the U.S. government would need to take in order to normalize diplomatic and economic relations with Vietnam.)

On March 2, 1977, the administration relaxed slightly restrictions against trade by allowing foreign ships and planes that called in or were bound for Vietnam to refuel in the United States. Restrictions on U.S. travel to Vietnam were allowed to expire on March 18, 1977. President Carter sent a commission, led by Leonard Woodcock, to Vietnam in March 1977 to discuss matters affecting mutual interests. On April 15, the U.S. Postal Service announced that it would accept for mailing to Vietnam standard postcards, letters, and small packages. And some progress was made on the MIA question when Vietnam returned the remains of 11 U.S. servicemen in March 1977.

The administration agreed to talks on establishing normal diplomatic relations in May and June 1977. During these talks, U.S. negotiators announced that the United States would no longer veto Vietnam's application for U.N. membership. (On July 20, 1977, the U.N. Security Council recommended by consensus without formal vote that Vietnam be admitted to the United Nations). The U.S. side proposed that diplomatic relations quickly be established between the United States and Vietnam, after which the United States would lift export and asset controls with Vietnam. But the Vietnamese said in response that they would not agree to establish relations or to furnish information on U.S. MIAs until the United States pledged to provide several billion dollars in postwar reconstruction aid. They later modified this position and provided some more information on MIAs, even though U.S. aid was not forthcoming.

The Congress, for its part, responded unfavorably to the Carter administration initiatives and the Vietnamese response. Members were particularly opposed to Vietnam's insistence on receiving U.S. aid. In the latter part of 1977, both Houses went on record as strongly opposing U.S. aid to Vietnam.

Developments in 1978 had a long-term negative effect on U.S.-Vietnamese relations. Vietnam expelled hundreds of thousands of its citizens (many of Chinese origin) as refugees throughout Southeast Asia; aligned itself economically and militarily with the USSR; and invaded Cambodia, deposing the pro-Chinese Khmer Rouge regime, and imposing a puppet Cambodian government backed by over 100,000 Vietnamese troops. The Carter administration halted consideration of improved relations with Vietnam. It worked closely with the members of the Association of Southeast Asian Nations (ASEAN) to condemn and contain the Vietnamese expansion and to cope with the influx of refugees from Indochina. The United States was particularly concerned with helping to support Thailand, a U.S. ally and the country most seriously affected by the Vietnamese invasion of Cambodia. U.S. officials also worked closely in this regard with other affected regional powers, notably China.

Developments During the Reagan and Bush Administrations

The Reagan administration opposed normal relations with Hanoi until Vietnamese forces withdrew from Cambodia. As Vietnam carried out substantial troop withdrawals from Cambodia, beginning in 1988, more emphasis was placed on the need for Vietnam to contribute to a peace settlement in Cambodia. Administration officials also noted for many years that progress toward normal relations would remain difficult until Vietnam gave a full accounting for U.S. MIAs. During periodic votes at the United Nations, the United States supported the Cambodian coalition government representing the guerrillas resisting the Vietnamese occupation. In 1985, Congress took the initiative and authorized the administration to provide annually up to $5 million in economic or military assistance in FY1986 and FY1987 to noncommunist Cambodian guerrillas resisting the Vietnamese occupation. Similar legislation passed the Congress in succeeding years. The administration also reportedly provided even more covert aid to the noncommunist resistance groups during that time. U.S. policy continues to reject any support for or direct contacts with the Communist Khmer Rouge guerrillas, who are loosely aligned with the noncommunist guerrillas in the coalition government resisting the Vietnamese occupation of Cambodia (see Appendix C).

Regarding the issue of the MIAs, Vietnam over the past few years has increased the pace of returns of the remains of Americans and Laos has also been more forthcoming in this area. There is a persistent belief in the United States that Hanoi holds more remains. A Vietnamese refugee testified before Congress in the late 1970s that the remains of several hundred Americans were stored in a Hanoi warehouse mortuary. Belief that living Americans are still in Vietnamese captivity also has grown in recent years amid reports from former U.S. government officials and others testifying to this possibility.[4] Hanoi denies that it holds living Americans or the remains of U.S. MIAs. The Reagan administration released a report in January 1989 that noted the difficulty involved in ever obtaining a full accounting of MIAs in Indochina. President Bush's inaugural address alluded to the MIA issue, pledged that assistance in this area would be long remembered, and called on Americans to put the divisiveness of the Vietnam war behind them.

Other humanitarian issues of interest to the United States have prompted U.S. efforts to negotiate with Vietnam in order to:

- facilitate emigration from Vietnam of relatives of Vietnamese-Americans or permanent Vietnamese residents of the United States;
- regularize the flow of Vietnamese immigrants to the United States and other countries under the so-called Orderly Departure Program managed by the U.N. High Commissioner for Refugees;

- resolve the issue of the estimated several thousand Amerasian children (whose fathers are Americans and whose mothers are Vietnamese) who reportedly wish to emigrate from Vietnam to the United States;

- obtain release from Vietnamese prison camps and the opportunity to immigrate to the United States of an estimated many thousand Vietnamese who worked for the United States in South Vietnam or were otherwise associated with the U.S. war effort there.

On July 28, 1989, President Bush summed up the U.S. posture toward Vietnam when he said:

We look forward to normalizing our relations with Vietnam, once a comprehensive settlement has been achieved in Cambodia. That settlement must include genuine power sharing with the noncommunist Cambodians led by Prince Sihanouk and in internationally verified troop withdrawal. But Hanoi must clearly understand that, as a practical matter, the pace and scope of this process will be directly affected by the seriousness of their cooperation on POW/MIA and other humanitarian issues.[5]

Recent U.S.-Vietnamese Contacts on Humanitarian Issues, Cambodia

The administration and members of Congress have shown strong interest in contacts, including high-level diplomatic exchanges, with Vietnam. These contacts have focused on exploring signs of Vietnamese flexibility concerning humanitarian issues dividing the two countries, especially the accounting for the U.S. MIAs. Regarding Cambodia, the Bush Administration in mid-1990 took the initiative to begin talks with Vietnamese officials in order to seek peace in Cambodia.

In 1985, Vietnam prompted increased U.S. interest when it returned the remains of 30 American war dead, allowed the United States for the first time to carry out a jointly monitored excavation of a suspected B-52 crash site near Hanoi, and promised to settle the MIA issue by 1987.

In January 1986, a high-level U.S. official delegation went to Hanoi for two days of talks with senior Vietnamese officials. U.S. officials also spoke with the Vietnamese in Hanoi, at the United Nations, and elsewhere regarding other humanitarian issues of concern to the United States.

The pace of U.S.-Vietnamese contacts over the MIAs and other humanitarian issues slowed during 1986 and 1987.

On August 1-3, 1987, an official U.S. delegation led by retired U.S. General and former Chairman of the Joint Chiefs of Staff John Vessey, a special representative of President Reagan, visited Hanoi to discuss humanitarian issues. This marked the first such high-level U.S. visit to Vietnam since Leonard Woodcock traveled there for President Carter in 1977.

Subsequently, Hanoi renewed discussions to resolve MIA cases, allowed U.S. representatives to resume interviews of prospective Vietnamese immigrants under the U.N.-sponsored Orderly Departure Program, and held talks with U.S. representatives on possible immigration to the United States of some Vietnamese children fathered by American servicemen during the war, and of former prison detainees associated with the U.S. war effort in Vietnam prior to 1975. Laos also renewed efforts to settle MIA cases. The Reagan administration for its part officially acknowledged U.S. interest in meeting some of the Vietnamese humanitarian needs stemming from the war, dispatched a medical team to survey needs for rehabilitation of those crippled because of war injuries, and encouraged private U.S. groups to provide humanitarian assistance to the Vietnamese. Progress in late 1988 and 1989 included the dispatch of several U.S.-Vietnamese teams in Vietnam to search crash sites for MIA remains, and Vietnam's transfer to the United States of sets of remains said to be those of U.S. servicemen. In October 1989, General Vessey returned to Hanoi for a second visit to encourage forward movement on humanitarian issues. Progress on MIA issues appeared to slow in early 1990, but developments in Cambodia--notably a reported rise in power of the Khmer Rouge--prompted U.S. officials in Congress and the administration to press for U.S. contacts with Hanoi over peace in

Cambodia. The Bush Administration began talks with Vietnamese officials on Cambodia in August 1990.

Policy Options

The debate over U.S. policy toward Vietnam has focused on two broad and incompatible policy options. The changes in Vietnam's policies, especially the troop withdrawals from Cambodia and greater flexibility on the MIA issue, have prompted some in Congress and elsewhere to prod the administration to show greater flexibility in using diplomatic, economic, and other instruments to encourage further change in Vietnam's policies in accord with U.S. interests. But others disagree. They remain skeptical of the durability of the Vietnamese changes and deeply suspicious of Hanoi's intentions. They oppose such U.S. initiatives unless the Vietnamese meet preconditions involving a full accounting for MIAs and a peace settlement in Cambodia that is in accord with U.S. interests.[6]

It is important to note that the balance between these two groups has been and presumably will remain subject to change as a result of perceived changes affecting the two major issues in U.S.-Vietnamese relations: the situation in Cambodia and the MIA issue. Thus, for example, some members of Congress who oppose U.S. flexibility now might favor it later if Vietnam is flexible on a Cambodian settlement and continues to return remains thought to be U.S. MIAs. Or rising concern by some policymakers about the possible expansion of Khmer Rouge control of Cambodia as the Vietnamese withdraw might cause them to reassess U.S. policy toward Vietnam. Some might see residual Vietnamese influence (exerted perhaps through the PRK or some other means) as preferable to a possible power vacuum that would allow the Khmer Rouge to return. And they might wish to improve contacts with Hanoi in order to be in a position to help negotiate such an arrangement.

Of course, changes could move U.S. opinion in the opposite direction. In 1988, Hanoi briefly slowed its cooperation on MIA issues to show its displeasure with a U.S. policy statement on Indochina. This action reportedly prompted congressional sponsors of a resolution calling for the establishment of a U.S. interests section in Hanoi to postpone consideration of this measure for the rest of the 100th Congress.

Greater U.S. Flexibility Toward Vietnam

Proponents of this view hold that current policy changes in Vietnam indicate that U.S. policy should balance U.S. pressure against

Vietnam with positive diplomatic and economic policy overtures. Such initiatives include the following:

- Establishing a U.S. technical office, interests section or some other diplomatic presence in Vietnam to facilitate interchange over humanitarian or other issues.

- Easing of the U.S. economic embargo.

- Providing small amounts of food aid for Vietnam.

- Making stronger U.S. diplomatic efforts to help meet Vietnamese concerns about the return of pro-Chinese Khmer Rouge to power in Cambodia as the Vietnamese withdraw.

The first three initiatives are fully within U.S. power. While they are seen to have little direct substantive impact on conditions in Vietnam, they are viewed by some as important symbolic steps which would substantially undercut the international effort to isolate Vietnam diplomatically and economically on account of its military occupation of Cambodia.

The fourth initiative would depend on the U.S. ability to influence Thai and Chinese policies towards the Khmer Rouge (China is the sole source of supply for the group and Thailand provides sanctuary for the Khmer Rouge guerrilla bands). This ability, although hard to measure, would be considered more effective if it were associated with a broad international effort to press Beijing and Bangkok to cut off support for the Khmer Rouge.

According to proponents of this view, U.S. gestures toward Vietnam could result in several benefits:

- They could establish a more positive atmosphere in U.S.-Vietnamese relations that is more conducive to further Vietnamese flexibility on the MIA question and other humanitarian issues than the past practice of U.S. pressure. The Vietnamese leadership is perceived as highly nationalistic, divided over the scope and pace of changes in domestic and foreign policies, and therefore unable and unwilling to compromise in the face of unmitigated outside pressure. By balancing continued pressure with some positive gestures, it is argued, the United States would encourage "reformers" in Hanoi and allow the Vietnamese to "save face" as they seek to end Vietnam's international isolation through accommodation with the United States over humanitarian and other issues.

- U.S. flexibility could also encourage the Vietnamese to seek a compromise settlement in Cambodia acceptable to them and the United States. According to this view, such a settlement would involve the withdrawal of Vietnamese forces, restrictions on the Khmer Rouge, and the establishment of an ostensibly neutral coalition government that would not be threatening to Vietnam, Thailand, or other members of ASEAN.

- Such a settlement, in turn, could prompt China to moderate its hardline posture toward Vietnam--a development that would remove Vietnam's main reason for a close strategic alliance with the USSR.

- And, U.S. trade or investment with Vietnam could encourage greater western and Japanese involvement in the Vietnamese economy, reduce the economic imperative behind Vietnamese-Soviet relations and possibly lead to greater political reform in the country.

This course of events, it is argued, would see a notable improvement in U.S.-Vietnamese relations, a relaxation of tensions in Indochina and Southeast Asia, a possible reassertion of Vietnamese independence and nationalism against the USSR, and a curb on Soviet access to military bases in Vietnam. The latter is seen as important to the United States in light of the uncertainty that surrounds continued U.S. access to bases in the Philippines.

Continued U.S. Pressure Until Vietnam Meets U.S. Terms

Proponents of this view strongly oppose U.S. efforts to improve relations or ease tensions with Hanoi until the Vietnamese completely withdraw their forces from Cambodia, help settle the conflict there and offer a full accounting of American MIAs. In particular, they argue strongly against establishing a U.S. liaison office or interests section in Hanoi, easing the U.S. economic embargo, or providing U.S. aid until Hanoi meets U.S. conditions on Cambodia and the MIAs. They support restrictions on the Khmer Rouge because of longstanding U.S. opposition to the Cambodian communists' brutal rule, not out of an interest to meet Vietnamese concerns. These Americans often reflect a deep suspicion of Vietnamese leaders. They judge that the recent changes seen in Vietnamese policies are largely tactical efforts to cope with current pressures. If those pressures ease prematurely, it is argued, Vietnamese officials will revert to policies contrary to U.S. interests.

According to this view, Vietnam could move to exploit U.S. gestures to improve relations and ease pressure in ways detrimental to U.S. interests. In particular they maintain that:

- Such U.S. gestures could make the Vietnamese more difficult to deal with on the MIA issue. For example, it could confirm Vietnam's belief that holding remains of U.S. servicemen gives Hanoi considerable leverage over the United States, rewarding and reinforcing Hanoi's demonstrated tendency to use this leverage cynically, to gain greater concessions from the United States. Thus, under these circumstances, it is argued, the Vietnamese might be expected to stress past demands for U.S. reconstruction aid as a precondition for a full accounting on MIAs.

- Such steps would make it more difficult for the U.S. government to persuade groups in the United States, Japan, Western Europe, and international organizations who are inclined to offer assistance to Vietnam to refrain from such assistance. Some who are deterred for the present by the strong, U.S.-backed pressure against Vietnam might change their policy if U.S. policy changed. Increased international aid at this time, it is argued, could weaken Hanoi's resolve to change its repressive and expansionist policies.

- Easing U.S. pressure against Vietnam under current circumstances could exacerbate important differences of opinion among Asian states opposed to the Vietnamese occupation of Cambodia. For example, some claim that Indonesia could be expected to follow such signs of U.S. moderation with efforts of its own to seek a compromise political settlement that might legitimize Vietnam's continued domination of Cambodia. In contrast, China might respond by arguing for a continued firm international stance against Vietnam, and might view the U.S. steps as another in a series of recent negative features of U.S.-Chinese relations.

- More broadly, it is claimed by some that U.S. accommodation of Vietnam under current circumstances would reinforce what these observers see as a general image of the United States as weak and unwilling to stand fast over time, an image given credence, in their view, by the U.S. military defeat in Vietnam.

Proponents of this view judge that whatever signs of Vietnamese flexibility have appeared regarding Cambodia and humanitarian issues have been prompted largely by continued U.S.-backed pressure. To be effective, the United States must continue to do its part to apply this pressure until Vietnam meets U.S. conditions. Easing up now, they assert, would only further complicate U.S. efforts to get a full accounting for MIAs and to restore stability and peace to Cambodia and Southeast Asia.

Notes

1. A main source for assessing the U.S. policy debate on these questions has been the author's regular participation in the periodic meetings over the last three years of the Indochina Forum of the Aspen Institute in Washington, D.C. For further background on the debate, see the Suggested Readings, below.

2. See the *Washington Post*, June 8, 1990, p. 1.

3. According to the National League of Families (NLF), (from a telephone interview to a spokesperson at NLF, Washington, DC: November 7, 1989) in the two years following the visit to Hanoi by a U.S. presidential delegation led by John Vessey, Vietnam returned 230 sets of remains said to be those of U.S. MIAs. As of early November 1989, 78 of these were confirmed as those of Americans. From 1974 to 1987, Vietnam returned the remains of 174 Americans.

4. See Robert Goldich, "POWs and MIAs in Indochina and Korea: Status and Accounting Issues" (CRS Issue Brief 88061).

5. Message of President Bush to the National League of Families, July 28, 1989.

6. For an example of these contrasting views, see Congressman Chet Atkins, "Normalize Relations with Vietnam," *Washington Post*, September 27, 1989; and Senator John McCain, "Don't Reward Vietnam's Bad Faith," *Washington Post*, October 8, 1989.

5

Conclusion: Difficulties Facing U.S. Leadership in Indochina

Developments in 1990 appear likely to increase America's importance among the contending groups involved in the Cambodian situation. The Soviet Union, China and Vietnam all face massive internal difficulties. For the USSR and Vietnam, improved relations with the United States appear critical to their economic development. The hardline leaders in China also repeatedly reaffirm their interest in sustaining good relations, especially economic relations, despite fundamental Sino-American differences stemming from the Beijing regime's crackdown on political dissent. None of these communist powers would like to see their interests in improved or sustained relations with the United States adversely affected by differences over the Cambodian situation.

Japan has the economic power to exert an important independent influence in Indochina. But at least for the time being, the Japanese government has chosen to work in tandem with the United States. It has followed a U.S. lead in international financial institutions and other forums as far as aid to Vietnam and Cambodia are concerned. The ASEAN countries also remain solicitous of U.S. views and seek to persuade the United States to pursue policies seen by them as in the best interests of ASEAN and the United States.

Despite Washington's growing importance in dealing with the Cambodian situation, Americans leaders remain divided or otherwise reluctant to establish a firm U.S. leading position in seeking to resolve the Cambodian situation. Dilemmas that have vexed U.S. policy in recent years remain. In particular:

- U.S. policymakers are having difficulty establishing a proper balance between their desire to prevent Vietnamese domination of Cambodia and their opposition to spread of Khmer Rouge influence.
- They have yet to determine if the conditions in Cambodia and progress on U.S.-Vietnamese bilateral humanitarian issues have

reached a point where the United States can move decisively to normalize relations with Vietnam.

- They are having difficulty assessing the sometimes conflicting signals coming from our ally, Thailand, and other members of ASEAN about an appropriate U.S. policy toward Cambodia and Vietnam. Thus, the Thai prime minister and some other leaders in ASEAN appear at times to favor rapid normalization with both Phnom Penh and Hanoi; but others in Thailand and elsewhere in ASEAN urge U.S. caution in the interests of seeking a comprehensive peace settlement in Cambodia over the course of the next year or two.

- The United States is in the midst of adjusting to the changes in Asia brought about by the collapse of communist regimes in Eastern Europe; the Soviet communist party's willingness to end its monopoly power in the USSR; the rise of a more collaborative than contentious U.S.-Soviet relationship; and a decline in U.S. positive attention to China as result of differences since 1989. The outcome of these events remains unclear, as do their implications for the situation in Cambodia and Vietnam and U.S. interests there.

In particular, events in Eastern Europe and changes in East-West relations are likely to free U.S. government resources from the defense budget; but there is no guarantee that these resources could be put to use, through greater foreign aid or other means, to support a more assertive U.S. policy toward Indochina. Higher government priorities involve overall cuts in government spending, support for domestic programs, and foreign assistance to newly democratic countries in Eastern Europe and Latin America. International crises, such as that caused by Iraq's invasion of Kuwait in August 1990, have the potential to absorb U.S. attention and resources for an extended period of time.

Meanwhile, as U.S. leaders have begun in recent years to consider a less reactive, more assertive U.S. policy regarding Cambodia and Vietnam, they have examined more carefully possible American options. They have been unable to achieve consensus on them. Thus, for example:

- Some in the United States thought in the mid-1980s that active U.S. support for Son Sann's noncommunist resistance forces represented a good way to encourage the formation of a viable noncommunist alternative to the two more powerful Cambodian communist groups, the Khmer Rouge and the PRK.

But closer examination and battlefield experience showed severe leadership and morale problems in Son Sann's organization.

- U.S. attention then focused on Prince Sihanouk and his forces. The prince was seen by some to have great residual popular support in Cambodia; he could provide an effective check to the Khmer Rouge and to the PRK in a future Cambodian government. But closer examination of the prince's mercurial behavior and his close ties to China made many in the United States suspect his ability to play a meaningful independent role.

- As the Vietnamese troops withdrew from Cambodia, American leaders gave more attention to the possible growth of Khmer Rouge power and influence. Some in the U.S. Congress and elsewhere called for U.S. efforts to normalize relations with the PRK and with Vietnam in the interests of strengthening forces that would prevent a Khmer Rouge revival and possible takeover in Cambodia. But subsequent developments raised doubts about the credibility of Phnom Penh and Hanoi concerning the degree of residual Vietnamese influence in Cambodia. Most notably, the PRK reportedly called upon Vietnamese troops to stop a Khmer Rouge assault in western Cambodia in late 1989 -- well after the Vietnamese claimed all their troops had been withdrawn.

- In 1990, many in the United States had hopes that meetings of the five U.N. Security Council members would lead to a framework for a settlement in Cambodia. Closer examination showed that the powers, as they agreed generally among themselves, still had a difficult task before them in persuading the competing Cambodian factions to come to terms in order to establish and implement a framework for a new government administration in Cambodia.

Domestic U.S. politics has also made it difficult for U.S. leaders to agree on an appropriate course of action regarding Cambodia and Vietnam. The legacy of the U.S. experience in the Vietnam war is widely seen to complicate current policy choices. It causes some to resist efforts by the Bush administration to provide lethal assistance to the noncommunist resistance in Cambodia. They argue that such a commitment could represent the start of a misguided military involvement similar to that seen in early U.S. involvement with South

Vietnam. The legacy of the U.S. experience in the Vietnam war causes others to resist calls for normalization with Vietnam or with the PRK. They argue that Hanoi has been repeatedly perfidious in past interactions, continues to hold remains of U.S. MIAs, and should receive no benefits from the United States until Washington's conditions are fully met. More broadly, it causes U.S. politicians to be hesitant to revive the emotional feelings and likely antagonistic debate that would be associated with a more assertive U.S. role in policy toward Cambodia and Vietnam. The potential risks of coming out politically bruised or battered from initiating such a debate are seen as large by at least some American leaders. By contrast, the dangers of not taking a leading role may be less serious from the point of view of U.S. domestic politics.

This does not mean to say that American leaders are unconcerned about the suffering caused by war in Cambodia, the poverty that prevails in both Cambodia and Vietnam, the continued outflow of people from both countries, and the possible return to power of the Khmer Rouge. But there are seen to be many uncertainties surrounding the situation in Cambodia and events affecting the balance of forces there. And divisive U.S. feelings over Indochina are seen by some as easily aroused by a more assertive U.S. policy posture. As a result, it has been difficult for U.S. officials in either the executive branch or the Congress to build a consensus behind a U.S. policy that goes further than the recent mix of modest U.S. policy actions to seek a resolution of the Cambodian situation and of U.S. differences with Vietnam.

Events in Cambodia and Southeast Asia could work to the advantage of the current modest U.S. policy efforts. A general consensus has been reached among the five U.N. Security Council members; they could succeed in persuading their respective clients in Cambodia to go along with a settlement; an interim administration backed by the U.N. could be established and U.N. monitored elections could be held and the results respected by each of the contending Cambodian Parties. The Khmer Rouge is seen as the main source of potential disruption. If China agreed to cut off supplies or otherwise press the Khmer Rouge, it is possible that they might fall into line or be isolated as a dissident resistance movement. The achievement of such a settlement in Cambodia would presumably open the way to U.S. normalization with Vietnam.

It is also possible that a resurgence of Khmer Rouge power or other events in Cambodia could impel U.S. leaders to take a more decisive leadership role in shoring up international efforts to prevent a return to power of these reviled Cambodians. (Some see the start of such leadership in the Bush administration's decision to begin talks with

Vietnamese officials regarding peace in Cambodia in August 1990, but others remain skeptical that the talks represent a significant change in U.S. policy.) Or pressure in Southeast Asia and elsewhere for establishing more normal relations with Hanoi and Phnom Penh could build to a point where the United States would move ahead with its own normalization efforts, despite the absence of a peace settlement in Cambodia. Other scenarios are possible.

For the present, however, it appears that U.S. leaders in the Bush administration are generally reluctant to take a much more assertive leading role in Indochina. They have focused hopes they have for a settlement, and the related issue of reconciliation with Vietnam, on what appears to be a step-by-step process of building consensus among outside powers concerned with Cambodia and then building consensus among the Cambodian factions. (The recent U.S. talks with Vietnam about Cambodia appear to be part of this process.) This process has made progress but still may take time. In the meanwhile, U.S. policymakers are very attentive to developments in the region, watching for events (such as a resurgence of Khmer Rouge power, or a change in Thai or other ASEAN positions) that might prompt adjustment or change in U.S. policies. U.S. policymakers are also sensitive to signs of strong domestic frustrations with U.S. policy toward Cambodia coming from the Congress, the media and elsewhere. Presumably they are prepared to adjust U.S. policy to take account of these sometimes strong political pressures. The U.S. government continues to play a strong role in efforts to deal with such humanitarian issues as the return of MIA remains, refugee departures from Vietnam, and assuring proper care and handling of Indochinese refugees, migrants, and other displaced persons; and it has shown new interest in dealing with human suffering in Cambodia.

Appendix A

Guide to Key Leaders and Organizations in Cambodia[1]

The United States has not recognized any government in Cambodia since 1975. Two successive regimes have existed in Phnom Penh since then. The Khmer Rouge (also know as Democratic Kampuchea -- DK) ruled under Pol Pot. In 1979, the DK was ousted by the Vietnamese-backed People's Republic of Kampuchea. (The PRK changed its name to State of Cambodia in April 1989.) In 1982 the Khmer Rouge combined with two other resistance groups--the National United Front for an Independent Peaceful, Neutral, and Cooperative Cambodia (headed by Prince Norodom Sihanouk) and the Khmer People's National Liberation Front (led by Son Sann)--to form the Coalition Government of Democratic Kampuchea (CGDK). The United Nations seats representatives of the CGDK, although some countries (primarily those in the Soviet bloc) recognize the State of Cambodia as the legitimate government of Cambodia.

State of Cambodia (SC) (Formerly the People's Republic of Kampuchea -- PRK)

The current regime, created in January 1979 after the Vietnamese invasion of Cambodia and subsequent overthrow of the DK government, is a Vietnamese-installed Marxist-Leninist regime. At its inception, it was monitored and controlled by Vietnamese advisers at every level of government; although overt control has decreased, the Vietnamese still influence State of Cambodia (SC) policies. Hanoi continues to provide technical and advisory aid to the SC, and, as the Vietnamese forces have withdrawn, the SC regime is assuming more responsibility for security. In the past, SC troops have been troubled by inexperience, poor leadership, and low morale. Recently, however, although the problems continue, the SC troops appear to have expanded and to have become a somewhat more cohesive and effective fighting force.

The SC has established administrative and political structures down to the local level, and SC leaders see themselves as the only legitimate, functioning government of Cambodia. Their close association with Vietnam has simultaneously assured their survival but left them isolated and developmentally fragile. Many regime leaders are former Khmer Rouge officals and victims of Pol Pot's purges in the late 1970s. They are fundamentally suspicious of the DK, wary of a DK return to power, and concerned about the possible recurrence of the policies that forced them to flee to Vietnam.

Heng Samrin

Present Position: Chairman, Council of State, SC (since June 1981)

Background: Peasant background ... joined guerrilla movement in 1959 ... allied with Pol Pot in early 1970s; rose to military commander in eastern Cambodia during Pol Pot regime ... broke ranks in 1978 to flee to Vietnam ... elected president of People's Revolutionary Council in January 1979 ... elected to Central Committee, Kampuchean People's Revolutionary Party (KPRP), and appointed to Politburo May 1981 ... elected general secretary, KPRP Central Committee, December 1981 ... cousin of Chea Sim, Chairman of SC National Assembly ... speaks only Khmer ... born around 1934.

Hun Sen

Present Position: Chairman, Council of Ministers (since 1985); Minister of Foreign Affairs (1979-1986 and since 1987)

Background: Major spokesman, leader of current regime ... peasant background ... joined Khmer Rouge in 1970 ... became KPRP member in 1972 ... broke with Pol Pot in 1977; fled to Vietnam ... elected to Politburo, KPRP Central Committee, May 1981 ... well traveled ... strongly pro-Vietnamese ... born around 1951.

Chea Soth

Present Position: Vice Chairman, Council of Ministers, SC (since June 1981)

Background: Broke with Pol Pot in 1974 ... First Ambassador to Vietnam (January 1979-September 1980) ... Minister of Planning 1980-1986 ... Member, KPRP Central Committee, since at least 1981; elected to Secretariat and Politburo May 1981 ... has traveled to Soviet Union ... born around 1928.

Tie Banh

Present Position: Vice Chairman, Council of Ministers, SC (since at least November 1987); Minister of National Defense (since August 1988)

Background: Parted with Pol Pot in 1974 ... appointed provincial chairman for military affairs and chairman of training section, Ministry of National Defense, January 1979 ... by March 1980 was director of military training department of the armed forces ... deputy chief of staff of army, 1980-1982 ... Deputy Minister of National Defense 1982-1984 ... alternate member, KPRP Central Committee, since at least mid-1980s ... Minister of Communications, Transport, and Posts 1985-1988 ... born around 1945.

Chea Sim

Present Position: Chairman, National Assembly, SC (since December 1981)

Background: Widely traveled ... of peasant stock ... joined revolt against Pol Pot in 1978 ... by December 1978 was vice president of Kampuchean National United Front for National Salvation (KNUFNS) ... Minister of Interior January 1979 - December 1981 ... member of KPRP Central Committee and Politburo since at least December 1981 ... born around 1932.

Khmer Rouge (Democratic Kampuchea - DK)

The Khmer Rouge, a communist resistance group with a Maoist ideology, is run by a small group of leaders whose ties go back over 35 years. Led by Pol Pot, Khieu Samphan, Ieng Sary, Ta Mok, and Son Sen, the Khmer Rouge is best known for having initiated an infamous campaign of genocide in which over a million people were killed during the four years (1975-1979) the group was in power. Khmer Rouge officials have recently moved to improve their public image and isolate SC forces by criticizing the excesses of the past, claiming to now embrace parliamentary democracy and free enterprise, and lowering Pol Pot's profile. The Khmer Rouge is a member of the CGDK, and Khieu Samphan, Prime Minister of the Khmer Rouge, is the CGDK's vice president in charge of foreign affairs.

Pol Pot and his associates seized control of Cambodia in 1975. They were overthrown in 1979 by invading Vietnamese troops and later regrouped in the remote southwestern region of Cambodia along the Thai border.   Although Khmer Rouge Prime Minister Khieu Samphan and Supreme Commander Son Sen exercise nominal control over their military troops, it is widely believed that they are still directly commanded by Pol Pot. Khmer Rouge forces, estimated at and 40,000, continue active guerrilla operations against SC and Vietnamese troops. They prevented the larger and better trained Vietnamese forces from consolidating the SC's control in Cambodia. The Khmer Rouge relies on China and Thailand for military assistance.

The Khmer Rouge is an important component in any Cambodian peace plan.   Beijing wants it included in any post-settlement government.   Hanoi and the SC, however, insist that Pol Pot and several close associates must not be allowed to participate in a settlement.   Prince Sihanouk hopes to dilute the strength of the Khmer Rouge by incorporating it in a quadripartite coalition. Some ASEAN members and many Western countries worry that Khmer Rouge forces, either as the strongest component of any composite government or as an exiled faction, might attempt to seize control of the country and return to their past inhumane practices.

Khieu Samphan

Present Position: Vice President in Charge of Foreign Affairs, CGDK (since 1982)

Background: Prime Minister of Khmer Rouge since 1979 ... traditionally regarded as figurehead who is controlled by Pol Pot ... has attempted to cultivate a moderate and pragmatic public image by emphasizing unity among the CGDK's three factions ... Prince Sihanouk's Secretary of State for Commerce in 1962-1963; has urged Sihanouk to play an active role in any future government ... studied in France during 1950s ... doctoral dissertation on Cambodian industrialization served as one of bases for DK's economic policies ... has admitted some "errors" in DK's genocidal policies of 1975-1979 ... disappeared in 1963; reappeared in 1971 as head of now defunct insurgent People's National Liberation Armed Forces of Kampuchea ... Deputy Prime Minister 1973-1979 ... DK head of state 1977-1979 before replacing Pol Pot as Prime Minister ... born July 27, 1931.

Pol Pot

Background: Most influential Khmer Rouge official, despite announcement in 1985 that he had left principal posts;

resignations viewed largely as political ploy to enhance Khmer Rouge's international and domestic reputation ... studied in France 1949-1952; participated in Marxist-Leninist movement there ... during late 1950s helped create Khmer Communist Party; worked as revolutionary in countryside during 1963-1970 ... named DK Prime Minister in 1976 ... generally considered person most responsible for DK's record of atrocities ... described by Asian press as charismatic but often inflexible and totally committed to Maoism, Marxism-Leninism ... history of health problems ... given name is Solath Sar ... brother-in-law of Ieng Sary ... born around 1925.

Ieng Sary

Present Position: Member, Coordinating Committee for Economy and Finance, CGDK (since 1982)

Has served as Khmer Rouge Deputy Premier for Foreign Affairs since 1975 ... once highly visible spokesman for Pol Pot, but since 1979 public profile has been eclipsed by Khieu Samphan ... lack of international exposure tied to DK efforts to enhance public image by reducing role of those closely associated with Pol Pot ... joined Communist Party while studying in France during 1950s ... taught in Phnom Penh from 1958 until going underground in 1963 to escape arrest ... may have lived in Hanoi until 1971 ... during early 1970s often traveled as special envoy from "liberated" Cambodia --based in China--to sympathetic countries; served as special adviser to then Deputy Prime Minister Khieu ... named to CGDK economy and finance committee despite having no known economic background ... married to DK Minister of Social Affairs Ieng Thirith, sister of Pol Pot's wife ... born around 1930.

Son Sen

Present Position: Member, Coordinating Committee for National Defense, CGDK (since 1982)

Background: Succeeded Pol Pot as Supreme Commander of the National Army of Democratic Kampuchea in September 1985 ... had served as Khmer Rouge Deputy Prime Minister in Charge of National Defense Affairs (1976-1979) and secretary general of the Supreme Commission of the Democratic Kampuchea Army (1979-1985) ... studied in Phnom Penh and Paris throughout 1950s ... during that time served as educator, political agitator; avoided arrest in 1963 by going underground with Ieng Sary ... surfaced in 1970s, as chief of staff of rebel Communist forces (now defunct People's National Liberation Armed Forces of Kampuchea) ... named member of CGDK coordinating committee for defense in 1982 ... a Cambodian; born in South Vietnam in 1930.

Sihanouk National Army (Armee Nationale Sihanoukienne--ANS)

The ANS was established in 1981 by Prince Norodom Sihanouk. It is one of two noncommunist groups opposing the SC government and its Vietnamese backers. Widely regarded as Sihanouk's personal army, the ANS is composed of about 18,000 men, based mainly along the Thai border. The National Army is nominally subordinate to the National United Front for an Independent, Peaceful, Neutral, and Cooperative Cambodia (FUNCINPEC), a political group established by Sihanouk. FUNCINPEC, however, is largely a paper organization staffed with intensely loyal Sihanouk supporters, many of whom also hold posts in the ANS. Both groups rely heavily on aid from China, ASEAN, and the United States.

Prince Sihanouk, who served successively from 1941 to 1970 as Cambodia's king, prime minister, and head of state, is widely viewed as the pivotal actor in any Cambodian solution. He retains western, ASEAN, and Chinese support, and both the Khmer Rouge and the SC claim that they support him as a leader of a neutral post-SC Cambodia. Sihanouk resides primarily in Beijing, but he travels widely to obtain military and financial aid and diplomatic support for his efforts to remove the SC government. He has met with SC Prime Minister Hun Sen; each of the resistance groups; and leaders in Beijing, Washington, Tokyo, Europe, and the ASEAN countries in an effort to coordinate a settlement.

Norodom Sihanouk

Present Position: President, FUNCINPEC (since February 1989)

Background: Widely regarded as flamboyant, mercurial ... named CGDK president in 1982; has resigned and resumed the post several times since then; recently took it up in February 1989 after stepping down in summer 1988 in protest of Khmer Rouge activities ... in past has used threat of resignation, other political ploys in attempt to coerce cooperation among CGDK's three factions ... unwavering support for political rather than military solution to Cambodia's problems ... in 1941 selected by father to ascend throne; in 1955 abdicated in favor of father ... named chief of state in 1960 following father's death ... deposed in March 1970; aligned himself with Khmer Rouge operating from China ... returned to Cambodia after 1975 Khmer victory; resigned one year later and was placed under house arrest; 17 family members killed during Khmer Rouge control of country ... exiled in 1979 following Vietnamese invasion ... born in 1922.

Norodom Ranariddh

Present Position; Supreme Commander (since 1985); Commander in Chief and Chief of Staff, ANS (since 1986)

Background: Second son of Prince Norodom Sihanouk ... frequently serves as intermediary, personal representative for father ... elevation to top of ANS largely believed effort by Sihanouk to position Ranariddh for succession ... tasked with improving relations between FUNCINPEC, ANS, and CGDK factions ... educated in France; received doctoral degree in international law from University of Aix-Marseilles around 1970 ... returned to Cambodia and worked with resistance leaders during early 1970s ... arrested; acquitted on charges of engaging in terrorism in 1971 ... returned to France in mid-1970s to teach at alma mater ... inactive in politics, resistance efforts until about 1981 ... may have some financial, business ties to Sihanouk's wife ... born in 1944.

Norodom Chakrapong

Present Position: Deputy Chief of General Staff, ANS (since 1985); FUNCINPEC Representative to Coordination Committee for National Defense, CGDK (since 1986)

Background: Fourth son of Prince Norodom Sihanouk; half brother of Norodom Ranariddh ... General Staff portfolio includes oversight of plans, operations, intelligence ... concurrently serves as commander of ANS 5th Brigade ... trained as Air Force officer but believed to have limited military operational experience ... has reputation for challenging Ranariddh for father's attention ... has been in and out favor with Sihanouk since late 1970s ... among family members placed under house arrest in 1973 ... throughout late 1950s, early 1960s, traveled as soloist for Royal Ballet of Cambodia ... nicknamed Prince Pat ... born in 1945.

Tiep Ben

Present Position: Commander in Chief, Joint Military Command, CGDK (since 1986)

Background: Has been regarded as Sihanouk's premier military leader ... has not served with ANS since assignment as number two in Joint Military Command, CGDK ... previously had served as ANS chief of staff and Commander in Chief ... experienced, skilled military officer ... willingness to work with KPNLF forces has irritated some ANS officials ... by 1974 was commander of Kompon Thom Province military subdistrict and provincial governor ... fled to United States following 1975 DK takeover; settled in California ... became active in the resistance movement in 1977 but had no official position until appointment as ANS chief of staff in 1981 ... returned to Cambodian border area one year later ... born around 1930.

Khmer People's National Liberation Front (KPNLF)

The KPNLF, one of the two noncommunist resistance groups, was established in October 1979 in opposition to the Vietnamese-sponsored Heng Samrin government. The KPNLF is led by Son Sann and a seven-member Executive Committee composed largely of men associated with former royalist or pro-western governments. The Khmer People's National Liberation Armed Forces (KPNLAF) is commanded by General Sak Sutsakhan.

In mid-1987 the KPNLF had only 5,000 troops; an expansion effort launched in mid-1988 brought its strength to a total of 12,000 to 14,000 by 1989. Most of these were new recruits, however, and no more than a few thousand are in Cambodia at any one time--the rest remain in Thailand. Son Sann admits that the KPNLF is no longer the strongest noncommunist force. It is dependent for supplies on the Chinese and ASEAN and complains that inadequate support is the primary reason for its lackluster performance over the years. While logistic support has been erratic, shortcomings in leadership and other organizational weaknesses are more serious impediments to its success.

The KPNLF is plagued by struggles for control of the military, and the squabbling has seriously hampered the leadership's military efforts, contributed to the loss of all major bases on the Cambodian side of the Thai border during past dry-season offensives, and eroded KPNLF political stature.

Son Sann

Present Position: President, KPNLF (since 1979); Prime Minister, CGDK (since 1982)

Background: Founder of KPNLF ... studied in France ... Prince Norodom Sihanouk's childhood tutor ... known to hold animosity toward Sihanouk ... since 1946 has served in many government positions related to economics, finance ... after Sihanouk's overthrow in 1970, retired to Paris and mediated between Cambodian factions for five years ... publicly criticized for divisive machinations to regain control of military, exacerbating bitter internal rivalries ... rival of other leaders who support Sak Sutsakhan's control of the KPNLF military forces ... born around 1911.

Sak Sutsakhan

Present Position: Vice President, KPNLF (since 1983); Commander in Chief, KPNLAF (since 1986)

Background: Minister of Defense under Norodom Sihanouk (1957-1959) ... chief of staff, Cambodian National Armed Forces, when government fell to DK in 1975 ... escaped to United States and lived there until 1981; then joined KPNLF on Thai-Cambodian border ... chairman (de facto chief of staff) of four-man Interim Military Committee, KPNLF, 1982 ... officially named Commander in Chief in 1984; two years later allegedly resigned, then was reappointed ... began placing his followers in high-level military positions in 1987 ... compatriots describe him as diplomatic but indecisive ... born in 1928.

Dien Del

Present Position: Vice President, KPNLF (since 1983); Deputy Commander in Chief, KPNLAF (since 1987)

Background: Joined Cambodian armed forces in 1956 ... promoted to brigadier general in 1972 ... fled to United States after 1975 DK takeover ... two years later went to France to work with Son Sann ... appointed chief of staff, KPNLF, in 1979 ... resigned in 1982 but resumed position three years later ... in 1986 Son Sann tried to fire him; by 1987 had been promoted to present post by

General Sak Sutsakhan ... wife and two children reside in United States ... ethnic Cambodian; born in South Vietnam around 1932.

Abdul Gaffar Peang Meth

Present Position: Deputy Chief of Staff for Planning and Psychological Operations, KPNLAF (since 1987)

Background: Described by Asian press as one of the brightest and most reliable individuals in KPNLF ... U.S. citizen ... Ph.D. from University of Michigan 1973 ... press and information officer at Cambodian Embassy, Washington, 1973-1975 ... helped resettle Cambodian refugees in United States after establishment of DK ... lived in Washington 1977-1979 ... worked for KPNLF committee 1979-1981 ... strong partisan of close cooperation with Sihanouk ... joined KPNLF team negotiating to form CGDK 1981 ... opposition to Son Sann led to expulsion from KPNLF the following year; currently serves under Sak Sutsakhan ... ethnic Cham Muslim ...born in 1944.

Notes

1.   This guide is taken from the Office of Leadership Analysis of the Central Intelligence Agency, "Guide to Key Players in Cambodia," Reference Aid No. LDA 89-11517.   June 1989.

Appendix B

**Procedural and Jurisdictional Questions Regarding Possible
Normalization of U.S. Diplomatic and Economic
Relations with Vietnam[1]**

This appendix reviews U.S. legal and regulatory restrictions on U.S. relations with Vietnam; addresses specific procedural and jurisdictional questions involved in normalizing U.S. diplomatic, economic, or other relations with Vietnam; and presents a range of possible actions the United States could take in key areas of diplomatic and economic policy if it decided to improve relations with Vietnam. This appendix does not address the pros and cons of possible progress in U.S. relations with Vietnam, which are discussed in the main body of this book.

Specifically, it first examines procedural and jurisdictional questions related to the normalization of diplomatic relations. It addresses the following questions: What is the current status of U.S.-Vietnamese political relations? Which branch of the U.S. government has responsibility for normalizing political relations? What are the different processes involved in establishing government-to-government relations? What are the procedures to establish an interest section or a liaison office? If the United States were to normalize diplomatic relations with Vietnam, what further steps might the United States consider undertaking?

It then examines some of the procedural questions related to the possible expansion of economic and commercial relations between the United States and Vietnam. Specific questions addressed include: the current status of U.S.-Vietnamese economic relations; what would be required for the United States to lift restrictions on U.S.-Vietnamese commercial ties; what would be necessary for the United States to implement other U.S. economic programs for Vietnam; and how the U.S. position on multilateral assistance to Vietnam might change with normalized relations.

It finally presents case studies on the different procedures the United States undertook to normalize diplomatic and economic relations with both the Soviet Union in 1933, and with the People's Republic of China from 1971 to 1979.

Questions Involved in Normalizing U.S.-Vietnamese Diplomatic Relations

What Is the Current Status of U.S.-Vietnamese Political Relations?

The United States has never recognized the Socialist Republic of Vietnam and presently recognizes no government as the sovereign authority in the territory known formerly as South Vietnam. The United States had not recognized the predecessor to the Socialist Republic of Vietnam -- the Democratic Republic of Vietnam (the communist government in North Vietnam). The United States did have full relations with the noncommunist South Vietnamese government until it fell to the communists in 1975.

In July 1989, President Bush stated as U.S. policy that the United States would not normalize diplomatic relations with the Socialist Republic of Vietnam until a comprehensive settlement has been achieved in Cambodia that would include genuine power sharing with the noncommunist Cambodians led by Prince Sihanouk, as well as an internationally verified withdrawal of Vietnamese troops. He added that as a "practical matter," the pace and scope of U.S. normalization will be directly affected by the degree of Hanoi's cooperation on POW/MIA and other humanitarian issues.

Although the United States and Vietnam do not have diplomatic relations, they have conducted direct negotiations on the issue of U.S. personnel missing in action (MIA) from the Vietnam War and other "humanitarian" issues stemming from the war.[2] U.S. and Vietnamese political leaders have also met to discuss issues of mutual concern at such international fora as the International Conference on Indo-Chinese Refugees, held in Geneva in 1989. U.S. officials met with Vietnamese officials to discuss peace in Cambodia in August 1990.

Which Branch of the U.S. Government Has Responsibility for Normalizing Political Relations?

The U.S. Constitution divides the foreign relations powers between the executive and legislative branches of the government. For example, the Constitution gives the President the power to send and receive ambassadors, while Congress has the power to regulate commerce with foreign nations, to define offenses against the law of nations, and to declare war. The President and the Senate share the power to make treaties and appoint ambassadors.

Although the Constitution does not ascribe the powers of recognizing states and governments to any particular branch of the government, the President traditionally exercises such privileges. The legislative branch of the government exercises little direct influence over the normalization of relations. Congress does control appropriations that might be necessary to implement the President's plan to establish relations.

What Are the Different Processes Involved in Establishing Government-to-Government Relations?

There are two general aspects to the process of establishing relations between governments: 1) recognition of a sovereign state, and 2) establishment of diplomatic relations. Governments can choose to recognize a state -- such recognition is accorded to an entity having a defined area and population under the control of a government that has the capacity to engage in foreign relations. Recognition of a state, however, does not necessarily mean the recognition of the government of that state. Oftentimes, political considerations influence a government's willingness to establish or reestablish diplomatic relations with the foreign state.

In a 1977 decision -- *Republic of Vietnam v. Pfizer, Inc.*, 556 F.2d. 892 (1977)[3] -- the U.S. Court of Appeals of the Eighth Circuit affirmed the dismissal of the case by a lower court, and noted in its opinion that, "the Republic of Vietnam, **both as a state and as a government** (emphasis added), had ceased to exist in law or fact and the United States had not recognized any government as the sovereign authority in the territory formerly known as South Vietnam." U.S. policy on recognition for Vietnam has not changed since that time.

What Are the Procedures to Establish an Interest Section? A Liaison Office?

In certain cases, the United States has maintained interest sections or liaison offices in countries with which it has no diplomatic relations. In the case of Cuba, for instance, the United States conducts business with Cuba through the U.S. Interests Section in Havana. The Interests Section is officially part of the Swiss Embassy, but is located in the former U.S. Embassy building. The Cuban Interests Section in Washington operates through the Czechoslovakian Embassy, although it is located in the former Cuban Embassy building. The State Department was responsible for negotiating the agreement with the Government of Cuba that led to the creation of the respective interests sections.

The United States maintained a liaison office in Beijing from 1973 until it established diplomatic relations with the People's Republic of China (PRC) in 1979. Until 1979, the United States officially had relations with the government of the Republic of China -- located in Taiwan. Upon establishing diplomatic relations with the PRC in 1979, the United States broke official relations with Taiwan.

Currently, U.S. commercial and cultural interaction with the people of Taiwan is facilitated through the American Institute in Taiwan (AIT) -- a non-governmental entity staffed largely by U.S. State Department and other officials who are temporarily separated from the U.S. Government. The AIT was established under the authority of the Taiwan Relations Act (P.L. 96-8, 22 U.S.C. 3301-3316). Section 7(a) of the Act authorizes personnel at the AIT to perform notarial, conservator, and consular services. Section 10(c) of the Act grants diplomatic status to the Coordination Council for North American Affairs (the Taiwanese liaison office in Washington), and to its personnel.

If the United States Were to Normalize Diplomatic Relations with Vietnam, What Further Steps Might the United States Consider Undertaking?

Cultural and Educational Exchanges

The United States has no official cultural, scientific, or educational exchange programs with Vietnam and has only very limited unofficial exchanges. If the United States were interested in pursuing such programs with Vietnam it might look to the U.S.-PRC experience as a model.

In January 1979, the United States and the PRC signed a Cultural Agreement that has established a basis for long-term official exchange. According to the agreement, the U.S. Information Agency is charged with managing the U.S.-China cultural exchange program. The agreement, however, governs only official, government-to-government contacts, and neither precludes nor covers other U.S.-China cultural exchanges that may be privately sponsored. As has occurred under many official U.S.-PRC agreements, costs of the official cultural exchange programs have been reciprocal, with each country covering the costs of its own involvement.

Travel Restrictions

Although the United States has no restrictions against U.S. citizens travelling to Vietnam, the State Department has issued a travel advisory for U.S. citizens going to Vietnam. Because the United States has no diplomatic relations with Vietnam, the State Department is not in a position to assist U.S. citizens travelling there.

Refugee Resettlement Agreements

The United States and Vietnam have had talks and reached agreements relating to the Orderly Departure Program (ODP) -- a program that facilitates the emigration of people from Vietnam with family or other contacts in the United States. In July 1989, the United States and Vietnam initialed an ad referendum agreement concerning the ODP, which dealt with a resettlement program for released reeducation center detainees. The United States hoped to begin interviews under that program in October at an initial rate of 1,000 people per month. The administration proposed that FY1990 admissions for both reeducation center detainees and Amerasian immigrants total 26,500, compared to the revised FY1989 ceiling of 22,000.

In 1989, the United States was also a participant in the International Conference on Indo-Chinese Refugees, held in Geneva. The countries participating in the conference endorsed a Comprehensive Plan of Action to curb the mounting flow of people from Vietnam. The conferees endorsed a strategy of screening Vietnamese emigrants and providing third country resettlement for political refugees only. The United States agreed that within three years it would accept 22,000 of the 55,000 Vietnamese refugees who have been occupying refugee camps in first asylum countries since before screening began. In addition, the United States agreed to accept one-half of all those Vietnamese emigrants determined to be refugees after screening began. In return, Vietnam has agreed to regulate the flow of emigrants out of the country.

Questions Involved in Normalizing U.S.-Vietnamese Economic Relations

What Is the Present Status of U.S.-Vietnamese Trade and Financial Relations, and What Measures Would Be Required to Normalize Such Relations?

Vietnam is one of the handful of countries whose economic relations with the United States are subject to a regime of U.S. sanctions of the most comprehensive and restrictive kind. In addition to an embargo on U.S. commercial and financial transactions with Vietnam, numerous types of transactions (various aspects of merchandise trade, export credits, private investments) are prohibited, limited, or subject to discriminatory practices by specific provisions of law and regulation. Most of these sanctions were originally imposed against North Vietnam in the context of the Vietnam conflict and expanded to include South Vietnam after its takeover by North Vietnam in late April 1975; a few have been applied on other, more specific grounds. If the United States were to normalize relations with Vietnam, it could lift some, all, or none of the restrictions on trade and financial relations with the Hanoi government. In certain cases, the United States has imposed selected trade and financial sanctions against some countries with which it has diplomatic relations. Apart from sanctions, U.S. economic relations with Vietnam are adversely affected by Vietnam's poverty, its international isolation as well as by other bilateral problems with the United States, such as Vietnam's nonparticipation in certain international entities (General Agreement on Tariffs and Trade, Multifiber Arrangement).[4]

The measures whereby U.S. trade and financial relations with Vietnam could be normalized would depend primarily on the type of authority under which the respective restrictions have been imposed.

Some are mandated by specific statute applying only to Vietnam, others by broader statutes affecting a group of countries (e.g., "communist," or other similarly described countries which include Vietnam either specifically or by implication). These may, moreover, contain an element of executive discretion, generally subject to statutory condition for its use. Finally, the United States has imposed restrictions under general statutory authorities that have been applied to Vietnam by executive decision in response to specific situations.

Consequently, certain restrictions could be removed only by an enactment that repeals the existing statutory mandate, others could be revoked by executive action as authorized by and subject to the conditions, if any, imposed by the statute, and others still might be repealed solely at executive discretion. All measures, of course, could be eliminated by specific legislation.

Embargo on All Transactions

The most comprehensive U.S. measure restricting economic relations with Vietnam is a virtually total and strictly enforced embargo on all U.S. trade and financial transactions with Vietnam. The regulatory mechanics of the embargo, administered by the Office of Foreign Assets Control (OFAC) in the Department of the Treasury, consist of a general ban on all commercial or financial transactions, which can take place only if they are permitted by regulation or specifically licensed by that office. Those transactions authorized by regulation are merchandise exports that have been licensed by the Bureau of Export Administration of the Department of Commerce under the Export Administration Act and related regulations. Thus, in practice, the Office of Foreign Assets Control exercises operational jurisdiction over U.S. imports from and financial transactions with Vietnam. Part of the embargo consists of the blocking of the Vietnamese assets in the United States.[5]

Certain types of marginal transactions are generally permitted, among them limited remittances to relatives in Vietnam, expenditures incident to travel to, from, and in Vietnam, and importation by tourists of items of limited value purchased in Vietnam. In some other instances, where specific licenses are required, they are issued by the office for certain types of imports from Vietnam (e.g., news materials by news media, small value gifts).

The United States imposed the embargo on North Vietnam on May 5, 1964 (29 F.R. 6010) during the escalation of the Vietnam conflict by adding that country to the list of countries subject to the already existing Foreign Assets Control Regulations (31 C.F.R. Part 500). The embargo was extended in the same way to South Vietnam on April 30, 1975 (40 F.R. 19202), after the fall of the South Vietnamese government. These regulations were put into effect--and subsequently modified in various ways--by the Department of the Treasury or the Office of Foreign Assets Control under the "national emergency" provision of section 5(b) of the Trading With the Enemy Act, (TWEA). Although the "national emergency" authority of the TWEA was repealed in late 1977 and replaced by the International Emergency Economic Powers Act (IEEPA) (50 U.S.C. 1701-1706), the measures taken in exercising such authority (e.g., the Vietnam embargo) have been continued in effect through annual Presidential determinations that such extensions are in the national interest of the United States. The latest such determination with respect to the Vietnamese embargo (as well as several other similar sanctions) extended the embargo through September 14, 1990 (Presidential Determination No. 89-25, August 28, 1989, 54 F.R. 37089).

The embargo on all transactions with Vietnam -- including the blocking of Vietnamese assets in the United States -- could be removed by executive action. This could be achieved in several ways: by instituting a policy of approving the required licenses under the existing regulations, by changing the restrictiveness of the regulations with respect to Vietnam or exempting it from their applicability, or, definitively, by removing Vietnam from the list of countries subject to the Foreign Assets Control Regulations (31 C.F.R. 500.201).

U.S. Imports and Vietnam's MFN Status

In addition to being embargoed as a part of the general embargo, U.S. imports from Vietnam are denied the most-favored-nation (MFN), or nondiscriminatory, status. In practice, this means principally that the United States assesses customs duties on imports from Vietnam at the high rates enacted by the protectionist Tariff Act of 1930 rather than at the substantially lower rates resulting from concessions granted by the United States in subsequent negotiations with other countries. Because of longstanding U.S. statutory policy, dating back to 1934 and at present stated in section 126 of the Trade Act of 1974 (19 U.S.C. 2136), and, in most cases, obligations under various international trade agreements, such concessionary rates are applied as a matter of general policy to imports from all U.S. trading partners.

This policy was changed by section 5 of the Trade Agreements Extension Act of 1951 (65 Stat. 73), which required the president to suspend the MFN status of most communist countries as a sanction against their support of North Korea and China, then in armed conflict with the United States. The suspension was implemented generally by Presidential Proclamation 2935 of August 1, 1951 (16 F.R. 7635) and specifically for "any part of ... Vietnam, which may be under communist domination or control" by Trade Agreement Letter of the same date with effect on Sept. 1, 1951 (16 F.R. 7637). The suspension, originally applicable to North Vietnam, was automatically extended to South Vietnam after its takeover by North Vietnam in late April 1975. The suspension is applied at present to Vietnam by General Note 3(b) of the Harmonized Tariff Schedule of the United States (HTSUS) (not codified).

Continued denial of the MFN status to "nonmarket economy" (NME) countries, including Vietnam, is required by section 401, as affected by sections 402 and 409, of the Trade Act of 1974 (19 U.S.C. 2431, 2432, and 2439), enacted on January 3, 1975. MFN status, however, can be restored to an NME country conditionally under the provisions of the Jackson-Vanik amendment and related legislation of the Trade Act of 1974 if the country maintains in force an acceptable emigration policy.

Restoration of MFN status would require first, either a presidential determination that Vietnam is in full compliance with the freedom-of-emigration requirements of the amendment, or a presidential waiver of such compliance if he has determined that such waiver will substantially promote the objectives of the amendment (19 U.S.C. 2432), and, second, the conclusion of a trade agreement containing the reciprocal grant of the MFN status as well as several safeguard provisions required by law (19 U.S.C. 2435). Such agreement requires congressional approval by concurrent resolution (19 U.S.C. 2437(c)(1)) -- a requirement of doubtful constitutionality in light of the 1983 *Chadha* decision of the U.S. Supreme Court. The conclusion of the trade agreement would also be highly unlikely, if not impossible, unless diplomatic relations were first established between the United States and Vietnam.

A related provision, contained in section 403 of the Trade Act of 1974 (19 U.S.C. 2433) and potentially affecting Vietnam, denies the MFN status to any NME country which the President determines as not cooperating with the United States in accounting for, repatriating, or returning the remains of U.S. personnel missing in action in Southeast Asia, as long as such determination remains in force.   Such determination, however, has not been made.

Vietnam also is denied the status of beneficiary developing country (BDC) under the U.S. generalized system of preferences (GSP) (Sections 501 - 505, Trade Act of 1974; 19 U.S.C. 2641 - 2645), which permits a substantial array of products of countries designated as BDCs to be imported into the United States free of duty. The denial of the BDC status to Vietnam is evident from Vietnam's absence from the list of designated BDCs contained in General Note 3(c)(ii)(A) of the HTSUS (not codified).

The extension of the benefits of the GSP to Vietnam would be subject to several special conditions applicable only to communist countries, namely, that the country: (1) have the MFN status, (2) be a party to the General Agreement on Tariffs and Trade and a member of the International Monetary Fund, and (3) not be dominated or controlled by "international communism" (19 U.S.C. 2462(b(1)). At present, Vietnam fulfills only the condition of IMF membership. Whether or not Vietnam is dominated by "international communism," would be a matter to be decided by the president at the appropriate time. Vietnam's eligibility for the GSP would also need to be considered in the light of the denial of such eligibility to any country that has nationalized or otherwise seized property of U.S. citizens without compensation having been made or in the process of being negotiated (19 U.S.C. 2462(b)(4)). Neither of these two restrictions of the GSP eligibility is waiveable.

U.S. Exports

The Bureau of Export Administration of the Department of Commerce promulgates and administers restrictions on U.S. exports of general commercial merchandise through the Export Administration Regulations (15 C.F.R. 769 - 799.2) under the authority of the Export Administration Act of 1979, as amended (EAA79) (50 U.S.C. Appropriations 2401-2420). The restrictiveness of controls applicable to exports to any country depends on the country group to which a country is assigned -- where the degree of restrictiveness is reflected in the number of products that require an individual "validated" license for each shipment (or group of related shipments) to a destination. The assignment of countries to their groups and the establishment of licensing requirements is done by the Bureau of Export Administration under statutory guidelines.

Vietnam is one of four countries[6] in country group Z, the group subject to the heaviest restrictions, amounting to a virtually total embargo on exports. The mechanics of the embargo consist of the requirement that virtually all exports to group Z countries must be approved by validated licenses, and of the stated general policy to deny all applications for them (15 C.F.R. 785.1).

The present status of export controls could be normalized in ways similar to those applicable to the overall embargo: by repealing the stated general policy of denying all applications for validated licenses for exports to Vietnam (15 C.F.R. 785.1) and handling such applications on a case-by-case basis with the same criteria that apply to the majority of U.S. trading partners, or by reassigning Vietnam from country group Z to country group V, which would constitute complete "normalization," or to country group Y, which would place Vietnam at the same level of control restrictiveness with the Warsaw Pact countries.

On the matter of commercial military exports, section 38 of the Arms Export Control Act (22 U.S.C. 2778) authorizes the president to designate those items that shall be considered as defense articles and defense services (the U.S. Munitions List) and to promulgate regulations for the export of such articles and services. The president delegated this authority to the secretary of state who has issued the International Traffic in Arms Regulations (ITAR), (22 C.F.R. 121-130). Section 126 of the ITAR declares that U.S. policy prohibits shipments of defense articles and services to or from 16 communist countries including Vietnam, East Germany, and Hungary, but not Yugoslavia. To allow commercial arms sales to Vietnam, this regulation would have to be modified to remove the prohibition, and U.S. policy would have to be modified to permit the Office of Munitions Control of the Department of State to issue licenses or approvals for the export of items on the Munitions List or related technology.

In the case of government-to-government military sales, section 3(a)(1) of the Arms Export Control Act (22 U.S.C. 2753) prohibits the

U.S. government from selling or leasing defense articles or services unless the president finds that the furnishing of such articles or services to a country or international organization would strengthen the security of the United States and promote world peace. Section 25(a)(8) of the Act requires the president to report to Congress annually a list of countries for which presidential findings are in effect. The president would have to make such a finding before the U.S. government could sell defense articles or services to Vietnam. The president did make such a finding for Yugoslavia in January 1973, and for China in January 1980, but has not made any such findings for the other communist countries.

Exports of Foreign Countries

Exports from foreign countries to Vietnam are to some extent affected by Transaction Control Regulations (31 C.F.R. 505), which, with some exceptions, prohibit a U.S. person to engage in any transaction in connection with the sale or purchase in any foreign country, and shipment to any country of the Soviet bloc, including Vietnam, of any merchandise subject to multilateral controls of the Coordinating Committee for Multilateral Controls (COCOM), or prohibited by U.S. munitions or nuclear control provisions.

This prohibition, originally promulgated in August 1954 and now maintained in force under the same authority and administered in the same way as Foreign Assets Control Regulations, was applied to North Vietnam on February 6, 1965 (30 F.R. 1284) and to South Vietnam on April 20, 1976 (41 F.R. 16556). Shipments to Vietnam are not permitted any exceptions. These restrictions could be removed in the same manner as the overall embargo.

Export Financing

Financing of exports to Vietnam through export credits is restricted or affected in several ways. Participation in any U.S. government program that extends export credits or export credit guarantees or insurance is prohibited to any nonmarket economy country -- hence also to Vietnam -- unless the freedom-of-emigration conditions of the Jackson-Vanik amendment and related legislation are fulfilled. The principal programs affected by this restriction are export credits and credit guarantees or insurance of the Export-Import Bank of the United States, and export credits of the Commodity Credit Corporation.

Moreover, the Export-Import Bank of the United States is specifically prohibited by its own organic law (sec. 2(b)(2)), Export-Import Bank Act of 1945, 12 U.S.C. 635(b)(2)) from engaging in any type of credit transaction (credit, credit guarantee or insurance) for the benefit of any "Marxist-Leninist" country, among them the Socialist Republic of Vietnam, unless the President determines that such transactions are in the national interest. A separate determination is needed for any Eximbank loan of $50 million or more. No determination has been made with respect to Vietnam.

The prohibition of access to U.S. government export credits and export credit guarantees or insurance contained in the Jackson-Vanik amendment could be removed by the president in one of the two ways provided for in that amendment for the restoration of the MFN status, except that congressional approval of the restoration of the access to export credit facilities would not be required. The removal of this prohibition, however, would not affect the specific prohibition of such transactions contained in the Export-Import Bank Act itself. Extension of Export-Import Bank credits and credit guarantees and insurance to Vietnam, now unavailable to Vietnam as one of the Marxist-Leninist countries under 12 U.S.C. 635(b)(2), could be authorized if the president determined (1) that Vietnam has ceased to be a Marxist-Leninist country, *or* (2) that such transactions are in the national interest.

Private Investment

Apart from the general embargo, there are no specific restrictions on U.S. private investment in communist countries, including Vietnam. Such private investment, if found economically feasible by the potential U.S. investors, is, however, somewhat discouraged by the prohibition, contained in the Jackson-Vanik amendment, of investment guarantees (provided for U.S. private investments in developing countries by the Overseas Private Investment Corporation -- OPIC) for investments in "nonmarket economy" countries. This prohibition applies to the countries (including Vietnam) to which the same amendment denies the most-favored-nation status and export financing (see above). Moreover, as part of the Foreign Assistance Act of 1961, the OPIC statutes, which in addition to investment guaranties and insurance, authorize also pre-investment assistance (financing feasibility studies, providing investment encouragement grants and loans), are subject to the same restrictive provisions that apply to bilateral foreign aid in general under that Act.[7] U.S. private investment in Vietnam would become authorized if the overall embargo were lifted.

Other International Aspects

Apart from its implications for the Hickenlooper amendment[8] and GSP eligibility, the issue of unsettled claims by U.S. citizens and firms against Vietnam for their property located in Vietnam that was expropriated by the Vietnamese government poses a practical obstacle to normal economic relations. Under an amendment to the International Claims Settlement Act, added as its Title VII (22 U.S.C. 1645 - 1645o) by P.L. 96-606 (Dec. 28, 1980), the Foreign Claims Settlement Commission received and adjudicated the validity of claims by U.S. nationals against Vietnam arising from losses due to nationalization or other expropriations of properties in Vietnam on or after April 29, 1975. As a result, claims amounting to almost $100 million have been adjudicated as valid by the Commission. While the law sets out the procedure for the payment of claims awards, it authorizes no appropriation of funds for this purpose. The awards would be paid from the sums realized under the claims settlement agreement that would need to be concluded between the United States and Vietnam.

Lack of diplomatic relations between the United States and Vietnam also prevents the negotiation and conclusion of any bilateral economic agreements (e.g., trade, claims settlement, investment guarantee) between the two countries. Vietnam's nonparticipation in the General Agreement on Tariffs and Trade and the Multifiber Arrangement prevents Vietnam from enjoying the benefits that participants in those compacts are obligated to extend (with exceptions) to each other.

Vietnam's accession to the General Agreement on Tariffs and Trade (GATT) would have to be approved by the GATT Council after Vietnam's application (which thus far has not been made) and a detailed examination of Vietnam's trade regime and recommendation by a GATT working party, a procedure usually taking several years. If Vietnam acceded to the GATT, the United States could avoid its obligations under the Agreement (e.g., the granting of the MFN treatment) toward Vietnam by taking recourse to GATT Article XXXV, which allows nonapplication of the Agreement between two parties to it if at the time one of them accedes to the Agreement either party does not consent to such application.

While Vietnam is not a party to the Multifiber Arrangement (MFA), providing ground rules for the international trade in textiles, it could become one on terms to be agreed between it and the countries now participating in the MFA. But even if it did not, the United States could conclude with it a bilateral textile trade agreement under the provisions of section 204 of the Agricultural Act of 1956 (7 U.S.C. 1854), assuming that there are no other obstacles to the conclusion of such agreement and to such trade.

What Steps Might the United States Take Should It Implement U.S. Economic Support Programs for Vietnam?

The U.S. government administers such bilateral economic support programs as foreign assistance -- both economic and military -- the Overseas Private Investment Corporation (OPIC), the Trade and Development Program (TDP), and P.L. 480 Food Assistance. If the United States were to normalize relations with Vietnam, it could establish some, all, or none of these bilateral economic support programs with the Hanoi government. The normalization of relations with Vietnam would not require the U.S. government to implement any of these programs. The United States has diplomatic relations with many countries that do not receive any assistance through these programs.

Foreign Assistance

Several impediments stand in the way of a U.S. foreign aid program to Vietnam. Prohibitions on foreign economic and military assistance to Vietnam exist in the Foreign Assistance Act of 1961 (P.L. 87-195), the Arms Export Control Act (P.L. 90-629), and in the Foreign Operations Appropriations Act, 1989 (P.L. 100-461).[9] The Foreign Assistance Act of 1961 and the Arms Export Control Act are permanent laws. The Foreign Operations Appropriations Act, however, is a temporary statute and applies only to programs in FY 1989. In the case of provisions cited below that affect Vietnam, most have been continued for a number of years in the annual appropriation measures.

Listed below are the general provisions that prohibit U.S. foreign assistance to Vietnam.

- Section 620(f) of the Foreign Assistance Act of 1961 prohibits the United States from providing assistance to any communist country (a list of which appears in the statute), unless the president determines that: (A) such assistance is vital to the security of the United States; (B) the recipient country is not controlled by the international communist conspiracy; and (C) such assistance will further promote the independence of the recipient country from international communism. Alternatively, the President may exempt a country from this restriction if he determines and reports to Congress that such an exemption would be important to the national interest of the United States. Vietnam is on the list of communist countries. Under this provision, assistance to Vietnam could occur with presidential certification.

- The Hickenlooper amendment -- section 620(e) of the Foreign Assistance Act of 1961 -- requires the president to suspend assistance to the government of any country that has nationalized or expropriated or seized ownership or control of property owned by any U.S. citizen or by any corporation, partnership, or association not less than 50 percent beneficially owned by U.S. citizens. Such suspension shall continue until the president is satisfied that appropriate steps are being taken to resolve the situation. The provisions of this subsection shall not be waived with respect to any country unless the president determines and certifies to Congress that such a waiver is important to the national interests of the United States. Although Vietnam is among those countries that have expropriated U.S.-owned property, the executive branch has not chosen to invoke the Hickenlooper Amendment against Vietnam.

- The Brooke amendment -- section 518 of the Foreign Operations Appropriations Act, 1989 -- prohibits the United States from expending funds appropriated by that Act to provide assistance to any country that is in default during a period in excess of one calendar year in payment to the United States of principal or interest on any U.S. foreign assistance loan. Since May 29, 1976, Vietnam has been in violation of the Brooke Amendment. Pursuant to this provision, if Vietnam does not repay its debt, assistance to Vietnam could occur only through legislative action.

- Section 620(q) of the Foreign Assistance Act of 1961 includes a provision similar to the Brooke Amendment. Section 620(q) prohibits any assistance to a country that is in default during a period of six months in payment to the United States of principal or interest on any U.S. foreign assistance loan, unless the president determines that assistance to such country is in the national interest and notifies Congress of such determination. Vietnam has been held in violation of this provision since November 29, 1975. Under Section 620(q), assistance to Vietnam could occur with presidential certification.

- Section 512 of the Foreign Operations Appropriations Act, 1989 prohibits the United States from expending funds appropriated by this act to provide any direct assistance or reparations to a series of countries. Vietnam is among those countries. Under this provision, Congress would have to delete Vietnam from this list of countries when it undertakes the annual appropriations legislation for foreign operations.

Beyond the options noted above to remove prohibitions through legislative action or specific waivers, the president could use his special authority under section 614 of the Foreign Assistance Act of 1961 (22 U.S.C. 2364). The section 614 authority permits the broad waiver of most statutory prohibitions on foreign assistance and allows the president to provide assistance -- up to certain limits -- to a country, notwithstanding any other provision of the act and other foreign policy acts, when the president determines that to do so is important to the security interest of the United States, and so notifies Congress in writing. The section 614 authority effectively gives the president the power to override prohibitions in the Foreign Assistance Act of 1961, the Arms Export Control Act, and a range of laws authorizing and appropriating funds for U.S. foreign policy, provided a credible security interest case can be made.

Because of the far-reaching nature of the section 614 authority, the President consults with, and provides a written policy justification to, the House Committee on Foreign Affairs, the Senate Committee on Foreign Relations, and the House and Senate Appropriations Subcommittees on Foreign Operations prior to exercising his authority. In practice, past presidents have used the authority sparingly and with close consultation with Congress.

Other Assistance and Financial Programs

Beyond these general prohibitions, listed below are prohibitions related to specific U.S. foreign assistance and financial programs.

Overseas Private Investment Corporation (OPIC): The purpose of the Overseas Private Investment Corporation (OPIC) is to provide political risk insurance for U.S. private capital investment in economic development activities in developing countries.

The authorizing legislation for OPIC constitutes a part of the Foreign Assistance Act of 1961. In most cases, the general prohibitions discussed above in the bilateral foreign assistance section would also apply to assistance provided through OPIC. Section 239(f) of the Act, however, might provide a model for enabling OPIC activities in Vietnam. It provides: "Except for the provisions of this title [containing OPIC legislation], no other provision of this or any other law shall be construed to prohibit the operation in Yugoslavia, or the People's Republic of China of the programs authorized by this title, if the president determines that the operation of such program in such country is important to the national interest." Establishing a similar provision for Vietnam could occur only through legislative action.

The president would also have to remove, with appropriate waivers or determinations, the prohibitions on U.S. government investment guarantees contained in the Jackson-Vanik amendment (removable by the same procedure that applies to the restoration of the access to export credit facilities under the same amendment).

Trade and Development Program (TDP): The purpose of the Trade and Development Program (TDP) is to promote economic development in Third World countries by supporting feasibility studies, consultancies, and training activities, as well as to stimulate U.S.

exports that might follow from the feasibility studies and other TDP planning services.

The authorizing legislation for TDP is also within the Foreign Assistance Act of 1961. The secretary of state has the authority to determine which countries are "friendly," for purposes of this program. If warranted, the Secretary could make such a determination for Vietnam.

P.L. 480 Food Assistance: Section 411 of the Agricultural Trade Development and Assistance Act of 1954 ("P.L. 480")(P.L. 83-480) specifically prohibits Vietnam from receiving U.S. food assistance through the P.L. 480 "Food for Peace" program, unless by an act of Congress assistance to Vietnam is specifically authorized.

Concessional sales of agricultural commodities under the Food for Peace program for foreign currencies and long-term dollar credits (sec. 101, P.L. 480) may be made only to countries which the president determines to be "friendly" to the United States. This term excludes "any country or area dominated or controlled by a foreign government or organization controlling a world communist movement" (sec. 103(d)). Determinations as to which country is "friendly" for the purpose of this program are made, under delegated authority, by the Secretary of State on a case-by-case basis, but could possibly be applied to Vietnam.

Multilateral Aid

Normalization of diplomatic relations would have no direct effect on the U.S. position on multilateral aid to Vietnam. In other words, there is no statutory mandate that requires the United States to vote against multilateral loans to, or contribute to organizations assisting, countries with which the United States has no diplomatic relations; nor is the United States required to support multilateral assistance to countries with which the United States has reestablished relations. However, by virtue of its membership in and contributions to various international institutions for economic assistance and stabilization, the United States is faced with the situation of providing assistance indirectly to communist countries like Vietnam that also are members.

In the case of the International Monetary Fund (IMF)[10], the Secretary of the Treasury is required to instruct the U.S. Executive Director of the IMF to "actively oppose" the use of any IMF credit facility by a "communist dictatorship" (not further defined, but presumably including Vietnam) unless the Secretary of the Treasury, upon request, at least 21 days before the IMF vote on approving such use, certifies and documents in writing, and testifies before the Senate Committees on Foreign Relations, and on Banking, Housing, and Urban Affairs, and the House Committee on Banking, Finance, and Urban Affairs, that the three conditions specified in the law have been met (22 U.S.C. 286aa(a)). Since these conditions involve only drawings from the Fund for certain limited purposes, Vietnam's use of IMF facilities for any other purposes must be opposed by the U.S. Executive Director, unless legislative authorization has been provided. The provision was added as section 43(a) to the Bretton Woods Agreements Act by section 804 of the Supplemental Appropriations Act, 1984 (P.L. 98-181, November 30, 1983; 97 Stat. 1270).

In the case of the multilateral development banks, current U.S. policy calls on the U.S. Executive Director to each of the multilateral lending institutions to oppose multilateral loans to Vietnam. This policy stemmed from a 1978 presidential directive by President Carter, citing U.S. concerns over human rights problems in Vietnam. Vietnam has not received any multilateral funds since 1978.

At some point, the United States might find it in its interest to discontinue its opposition to multilateral loans to Vietnam on the basis of current human rights or political objections. If this were to be the case, the United States would then be in a position to evaluate loan applications from Vietnam on economic and other criteria. Economic conditions in Vietnam are very poor. If the United States were to evaluate loans to Vietnam entirely on economic criteria, it might or might not continue to oppose multilateral funding to Vietnam. If political considerations were to outweigh economic criteria, the United States might find itself supporting loans to Vietnam that were less than economically sound.

In a related provision, Section 550 of the Foreign Operations Appropriations Act, 1989 (P.L. 100-461) prohibits any indirect U.S. assistance or reparations to a series of countries, including Vietnam, unless the President certifies that withholding these funds would be contrary to the national interest. The President recently made this certification through Presidential Determination No. 89-4 of October 20, 1988, 53 F.R. 44377. The prohibition on "indirect assistance" refers to multilateral aid to these countries and would effectively prohibit U.S.

contributions to any banks or organizations providing funds to these countries, absent a presidential determination.

Current U.S. law also affects U.S. contributions to international organizations that assist Vietnam. Section 526 of the Foreign Operations Appropriations Act requires that the United States withhold a share of its voluntary contribution to various U.N. and other international organizations in proportion to the amount of aid such organizations might have provided to communist countries listed under Section 620(f) of the Foreign Assistance Act of 1961. (See the discussion on section 620(f) above for details on how the President could remove Vietnam from the section 620(f) list.)

Procedures Followed by the United States in Normalizing Relations with the USSR and the People's Republic of China

There have been two important instances in which the U.S. Government normalized relations with foreign communist governments years after their actual ascendancy to power. In 1933--16 years after the Bolshevik Revolution-- the United States normalized relations with the Soviet Union. In 1979, the United States normalized relations with the People's Republic of China--30 years after the communist victory over the nationalist forces in 1949. These cases are reviewed below. They may indicate the types of procedures U.S. officials may consider if it were decided to move ahead to normalize relations with Vietnam.

Soviet Union (USSR)[11]

In 1917, President Woodrow Wilson responded to the Bolshevik Revolution by refusing to recognize the new Soviet government. Although the Soviet Union expressed interest in normalizing relations with the United States in the years following the Bolshevik Revolution, U.S. hostility towards communism in general and the Soviet government in particular precluded the United States from recognizing the Soviet government.

In the early 1930s, however, the United States found it increasingly difficult to ignore the permanence of the Soviet regime as well as the potential economic and diplomatic benefits of recognition. Despite the lack of formal relations between the governments, commercial ties between the countries increased somewhat in the early 1930s. In addition, U.S. concerns over the growing power of Japan in Asia and of Nazi Germany in Europe caused the United States to reconsider its stand on recognition of the Soviet Union -- especially since some U.S. officials felt that the Soviets might offer a strategic counterbalance to Japanese and German expansionism.

President Franklin Roosevelt was the key U.S. actor in the normalization process with the Soviet Union. As a first step, in May 1933, President Roosevelt included Soviet President Mikhail Kalinin among the European leaders he called upon to attend the London Economic Conference. In the spring and summer of 1933, the president also sent U.S. envoys to speak unofficially with Soviet officials on the issue of normalization. At the same time that he was taking these actions, the president worked to build public and congressional support for recognition. A growing consensus within the executive branch and Congress was that normalization should be contingent upon prior Soviet agreement to repay outstanding debts to the United States, and to cease its support of propaganda and subversive activities against the United States.

In November 1933, President Roosevelt ordered U.S. officials to prepare for negotiations with the Soviet Foreign Ministry on establishing relations between the two countries. State Department officials recommended to the president that three major issues be settled before the normalization of diplomatic relations: protection of the rights of Americans in Russia, severing of all Soviet ties with communist activity in the United States, and settlement of Russian debts to the United States. Moscow, on the other hand, preferred to address these issues after relations were normalized -- U.S. negotiators, however, refused.

After several days of unsuccessful negotiations between State Department and Soviet officials, President Roosevelt and the Soviet Union's chief negotiator, Soviet Commissar Maxim Litvinov, met to directly address the three issues. The president and Litvinov readily agreed on a guarantee of freedom of worship and conscience for American citizens in the Soviet Union. The final agreement also required Moscow to sever its ties with the American Communist party and other communist-controlled organizations in the United States. The Soviet Union also made a pledge not to permit the formation or residence on its territory of any organization or group which aimed to overthrow or prepare for the overthrow of, or bring about by force a change in, the political or social order of the United States.

Resolving the debt issue, however, was more problematic. In the end, the president agreed to a compromise accord. It was agreed that Russian assets in the United States that the Soviets were claiming for themselves and some other of their claims against the United States would be assigned to the United States. These assignments (in effect) of proceeds from liquidation of Russian assets were far from sufficient to pay off the debt. It appears that at the time of the negotiations, President Roosevelt viewed the resolution of the debt issue as a less significant barrier to normalized relations than did the State Department. The two negotiators appeared to pay little attention to administrative details, which later led to disagreements between the two countries over the interpretation of the agreement.

In the end, after appearing to have reached an understanding on these issues, President Roosevelt and Commissar Litvinov signed an agreement that same day which normalized relations between the two countries after 16 years of nonrecognition.

People's Republic of China (PRC)[12]

In 1949, the Nationalist government of Chiang Kai-shek fell to the communists on Mainland China and relocated to Taiwan. The United States continued diplomatic relations with the nationalists, while refusing to recognize the government of the People's Republic of China (PRC).

Despite the hostility between the United States and the PRC, the two countries did maintain face-to-face communications from 1955 to 1971 through so-called ambassadorial talks conducted by their respective ambassadors, at first, in Switzerland and, later, in Poland. Although little was accomplished through these communications, some officials contended that these discussions helped to prevent misunderstandings that could have exacerbated such regional issues as U.S. military support for Taiwan and the U.S. involvement in the Vietnam War.

In 1969 and 1970, the Nixon administration made several cautious moves toward increasing U.S. contacts with the PRC, by lifting certain travel and trade restrictions. In 1971, the State Department announced it had terminated all restrictions on travel to China. In addition, the

United States effectively lifted the U.S. trade embargo against China and reduced some export controls on goods to China.

In July 1971, Henry Kissinger made a secret trip to Beijing to lay the groundwork for future Sino-American relations. The two parties reached agreement on the following issues: 1) that Taiwan was part of China; 2) that the political future of South Vietnam should be decided by the Vietnamese; and 3) that all Asian disputes should be settled by peaceful means. At the time, the Chinese also extended an invitation to President Nixon to visit China. President Nixon later announced that he would travel to China in early 1972.

On February 14, 1972 -- the week before his departure for the PRC -- President Nixon ordered the reassignment of China from country Group Z to country Group Y with respect to U.S. export control policy.[13] This move placed China on the same level of U.S. trade restrictions as the Soviet Union and the Warsaw Pact countries. Furthermore, President Nixon directed the Treasury Department to remove the requirement that U.S.-controlled firms abroad obtain Treasury approval for the export of strategic goods and foreign technology to the PRC.

On February 21, 1972, President Nixon arrived in China for a week of consultations with Chinese officials. At the end of the visit, President Nixon and Chinese Premier Zhou Enlai released a joint statement -- known as the Shanghai communique -- agreeing that progress toward "the normalization of relations" between the two sides was "in the interests of all countries."

In February 1973, in an effort to regularize bilateral contact and lay the groundwork for normal diplomatic relations, the United States and the PRC agreed to open non-diplomatic liaison offices in each other's capitals. In April 1973, Congress approved legislation (P.L. 93-22) that extended diplomatic immunities and privileges to the staff of the liaison office of the PRC, when it opened the following month.

In October 1978, President Carter signed the Agricultural Trade Act of 1978 (P.L. 95-501) that contained a provision (sec. 202, 7 U.S.C. 1707c) allowing the Commodity Credit Corporation to extend short-term (up to three years) credit to the PRC. Previously, the PRC had been ineligible for such credit under the provisions of the Jackson-Vanik Amendment to the 1974 Trade Act.

In December 1978, President Carter announced that beginning on January 1, 1979, the United States and the PRC would establish diplomatic relations, and the United States would discontinue official relations with Taiwan. The exchange of ambassadors would take place in March 1979. The terms of the agreement called on the United States: 1) to recognize the PRC as the sole legitimate government of China, 2) to acknowledge that Taiwan was part of China, and 3) to end all official governmental relations with Taiwan and withdraw its troops from the island within four months. At the same time, the United States still could maintain and develop its existing nongovernmental relations with Taiwan on a "people to people" basis.

The final agreement involved concessions by both sides. The agreement allowed the United States to end its Mutual Defense Treaty with Taiwan one year later, which was stipulated within the original terms of the treaty. Second, Beijing did not contradict the unilateral statement by Washington that the United States "expects" the Taiwan issue to be resolved peacefully. Third, despite its objections, Beijing proceeded with normalization despite the announced intentions of the United States to continue to supply Taiwan with "defensive" weapons. For its part, Washington accepted Beijing's terms for normalization without any formal assurance that it would not use force to take over Taiwan.

In January 1979, Vice Premier Deng Xiaoping visited the United States and signed a series of agreements that: 1) provided for the establishment of consulates in both countries, 2) established an overall science and technology agreement, 3) authorized U.S. aid for building a nuclear accelerator in China, 4) entitled the PRC to launch a communications satellite through NASA, 5) established a cultural exchange agreement, and 6) provided for student exchanges.

In March 1979, the U.S. Treasury negotiated an agreement with the Chinese Finance Ministry, that was signed in May 1979, whereby claims by U.S. citizens in effect would be settled at 41 cents on the dollar.[14] The agreement enabled Chinese trade with the United States to proceed without fear of seizure of goods.

In July 1979, the United States and the PRC signed a three-year self-renewable trade agreement that established the framework for normal commercial relations between the two countries and paved the way for the United States to grant the PRC most-favored-nation (MFN) status, within the requirements of the freedom of emigration (Jackson-Vanik) amendment of the Trade Act of 1974. The trade agreement was signed, however, only after the United States imposed unilateral quotas on textile imports from China. The agreement entered into force on

February 1, 1980, after the President, on October 23, 1979, granted a Jackson-Vanik waiver and the Congress, on January 24, 1980, approved the agreement. The textile trade agreement was signed after prolonged negotiations on September 17, 1980, retroactive to January 1, 1980, and subsequently extended several times.

The presidential waiver also removed the Jackson-Vanik amendment obstacle to China's access to the full range of U.S. government export credits. In addition, the specific ban on extending Export-Import Bank credits to communist countries in section 2(b)(2) of the Export-Import Bank Act was waived by a presidential determination of national interest (45 F.R. 26017, April 17, 1980).

The waiver also removed one obstacle to China's access to the facilities of the Overseas Private Investment Corporation. The other obstacle was the general prohibition on foreign aid to communist countries in section 620(f) of the Foreign Assistance Act of 1961 (22 U.S.C. 2370(f)), which then provided for a national-interest waiver only under very restrictive conditions, which were unlikely to qualify China for the waiver. Therefore, an amendment to an existing statute was enacted (P.L. 96-327; 94 Stat. 1026; August 8, 1980) which, in effect, authorized OPIC operations in China if the president determined it to be important to the national interest (22 U.S.C. 2199(f)). Such determination (No. 80-25, 45 F.R. 54299) was made on August 8, 1980, and an investment guaranty agreement was signed with China and entered into force on October 30, 1980.

Meanwhile a review of export control policies by the United States as well as by the Coordinating Committee on Multilateral Export Controls (COCOM)[15] suggested the appropriateness of a further relaxation of U.S. policy on exports that required COCOM approval to China compared with those to the Warsaw Pact countries. Because of this differentiation, China was reassigned in April 1980 to a unique country group (group P). The policy of approving licenses for export to China of dual-use (economic and military) commodities, with specified exceptions, was instituted. In November 1983, China was reassigned to country group V -- containing the majority of U.S. trading partners outside the Western Hemisphere -- although exports to China of certain sensitive strategic dual-use commodities that would normally be licensed for export to group V may require extended review or denial.

As to its multilateral economic relations, the PRC became a member of the International Monetary Fund on April 17, 1980, replacing therein the Republic of China (Taiwan); acceded to the Multifiber Arrangement on January 18, 1984; became an observer in the GATT in 1982 and is currently being examined for GATT membership following the filing of an application in 1986 to resume the China seat in the GATT, abandoned in 1950 by the Republic of China.

Notes

1.   This section is taken from a report completed on November 30, 1989, by the Congressional Research Service (CRS Report 89-631F) and released by the U.S. Senate Foreign Relations Committee in late 1989. Entitled "Vietnam: Procedural and Jurisdictional Questions Regarding Possible Normalization of U.S. Diplomatic and Economic Relations," the CRS Report was written by Alan Yu, Vladimir Pregelj and Robert Sutter.
2.   John Vessey's October 1989 visit to Hanoi is an example of high level exchanges on humanitarian issues. To facilitate Vietnamese immigration to the United States under the Orderly Departure Program, some lower level U.S. officials spend several weeks at a time on detail working in offices in Vietnam.
3.   In 1974, in *Republic of Vietnam v. Pfizer, Inc.*, the Republic of Vietnam filed suit in U.S. court against various U.S. drug companies, alleging that they had violated U.S. anti-trust laws. When the Republic of Vietnam was defeated by North Vietnam in 1975, a lower court noted that in U.S. law that a foreign government not recognized by the United States could not maintain suit in a state or federal court.
4.   Of course, other countries, like China, are also not parties to the GATT, and others are not members of the Multifiber Arrangement.
5.   The value of these assets as of June 30, 1983, following a census conducted by the Office of Foreign Assets Control, was $150.3 million, virtually all consisting of Vietnamese accounts in U.S. banks. This amount does not include the interest accrued on these accounts since that date, which, according to information received from the OFAC, would raise the present balance to between $210 million and $215 million. In addition, the value of the Vietnamese Embassy building in Washington, also a blocked asset, has been estimated at between $3 million and $4 million. (Telephone conversation with a spokesperson at OFAC, Washington, DC: October 1989.)

6. The other countries are Cuba, Cambodia and North Korea.

7. See the foreign assistance section for a discussion of OPIC.

8. See below for details on the Hickenlooper amendment.

9. The Foreign Assistance Act of 1961 authorizes such programs as development assistance, the Economic Support Fund (ESF), the grant Military Assistance Program (MAP), the International Military Education and Training (IMET) program, international narcotics control assistance, disaster assistance, and anti-terrorism training. The Arms Export Control Act authorizes programs to provide grants and credits for military sales to foreign countries under the Foreign Military Sales Financing program. The Foreign Operations Appropriations Act provides annual funding for foreign aid programs authorized by these and other acts.

10. The IMF Board of Governors replaced the Republic of Vietnam (South Vietnam) with the Socialist Republic of Vietnam effective September 15, 1976.

11. The primary source for the following information is: Thomas R. Maddux, *Years of Estrangement: American Relations with the Soviet Union, 1933-1941* (Tallahassee: University Presses of Florida, 1980).

12. The primary source for this information is: "China: U.S. Policy since 1945," *Congressional Quarterly* (Washington, DC: 1980): pp. 5-18.

13. Those countries placed in Group Z are subject to the heaviest restrictions, amounting to a virtually total embargo on U.S. exports. The mechanics of the embargo consist of the requirement that all exports to Group Z countries must be approved by a validated licenses, and of the stated policy to deny all applications for them.

14. The agreed to Chinese settlement payment amounted to $80.5 million, while the amount of adjudicated U.S. claims against China for nationalized, etc., property was $196.9 million. While this did mean a settlement of 40.8 cents on the dollar, that amount was not mentioned in the agreement. The settlement amount was distributed to the claimants pursuant to the provisions of Title V of the International Claims Settlement Act of 1949 (22 U.S.C. 1643-1643k).

15. COCOM coordinates export control policies among the United States and its major allies.

Appendix C

Status of Military-Political Groups Active in Cambodia*

Leader/Name of Organization	Political Status	Foreign Policy	Est. Force Strength
Heng Samrin/Hun Sen People's Republic of Kampuchea (PRK) (communist-- also known as State of Cambodia	In power (supported) by Vietnamese troops**)	Pro-Vietnam Pro-Soviet	40,000-48,000 main force 50,000 organized militia 50,000 unorganized militia
Khieu Samphan Ieng Sary Pol Pot/ Democratic Kampuchea (DK) (communist -- also known as Khmer Rouge)	Member of the Coalition Government of Democratic Kampuchea (CGDK) which represents Kampuchea in the United Nations; maintains the foreign affairs portfolio in the CGDK.	Anti-Vietmese Close ties with China	35,000-40,000 well-trained, well-equipped

---

* Precise U.S. Government estimates of forces in Cambodia are classified. These general estimates were confirmed during a telephone conversation with the Department of State.

** Vietnam says all its troops left Cambodia by September 1989. China, Sihanouk and others claim that after September 1989 there remain tens of thousands of Vietnamese troops, "disguised" as PRK troops.

Status of Military-Political Groups
Active in Cambodia

Leader/Name of Organization	Political Status	Foreign Policy	Est. Force Strength
Son Sann/Khmer People's National Liberation Front (KPNLF) (noncommunist)	Member of the CGDK. Sonn Sann is prime minister.	Anti-Vietnamese Pro-nonaligned and noncommunist nations	12,000-15,000
Norodom Sihanouk/ Sihanouk National Army (ANS) (noncommunist)	Member of the CGDK. Sihanouk sometimes serves as president.	Anti-Vietnamese Pro-nonaligned (leader often resides in China and North Korea)	18,000-20,000

Appendix D

Contending Groups and Their Stance on a Peace Agreement

People's Republic of Kampuchea -- (PRK; also known since 1989 as "State of Cambodia") Backed by Vietnam and the U.S.S.R.

-- Links Vietnam's military withdrawal with cut-off of support for Cambodian resistance cut-fighters.

-- Calls for disbanding of Khmer Rouge army before elections for a new government are held. Stresses past Khmer Rouge "genocide" in Cambodia.

-- At least until recently, has called for continuation of PRK until elections are held.

-- Opposes use of international supervison that would "infringe" on Cambodian "sovereignty."

VS.

Coalition Government of Democractic Kampuchea (CGDK) (i.e., Khmer Rouge, Sihanouk, and Son Sann forces.) Backed by China and ASEAN. The United States supports Sihanouk and Son Sann.

-- Calls for unconditional, verifiable Vietnamese military withdrawal. Claims tens of thousands of Vietnamese troops are "hidden" in PRK army.

-- Calls for allowing Khmer Rouge to participate as part of four party Camodian government prior to election. Calls for scaling back, but not disbanding, Khmer Rouge army.

Coalition Government of
Democractic Kampuchea
(CGDK)

-- Calls for disbanding PRK and
CGDK once four-party government
is established.

-- Calls for strong international role
in monitoring Vietnam's
withdrawal, assuring peace among
competing Cambodian forces, and
guaranteeing free elections.

Appendix E

Key Country Indicators[*]

Vietnam

Area: 329,560 sq. km -- Slightly larger than New Mexico

Population: 66.8 million (July 1989) -- Annual growth rate 2.5%

G.N.P.: $12.6 billion; $200 per capita

Exports: $880 million (1987)

Imports: $2.19 billion (1987)

Major Trading Partners: U.S.S.R., Eastern Europe, and Japan

Military Forces: Over 1 million

Cambodia

Area: 181,040 sq. km. -- Slightly smaller than Oklahoma

Population: 6.8 million (July 1989) -- Annual growth rate 2.2%

GDP: $570 million; $90 per capita

Exports: $3 million

Imports: $17 million

Major trading partners: Vietnam, U.S.S.R. and Eastern Europe

---

[*] Source: Central Intelligence Agency. The World Factbook, 1989.

Chronology

April 1975   Khmer Rouge fighters defeat the noncommunist regime in Cambodia; Vietnamese communist forces defeat the noncommunist regime in South Vietnam.

May 1975   U.S. military forces used to free Americans from the merchant ship *Mayaguez* captured by Khmer Rouge fighters.

April 1976   Khmer Rouge announces formation of new government of Democratic Kampuchea (DK) with Pol Pot as premier.

April 1977   Khmer Rouge-Vietnamese border conflict escalates.

May 1977   Congress votes to prohibit any U.S. reparations or aid to Vietnam.

July-Sept. 1977   Further Vietnamese-Cambodian border tensions.

October 1977   Vietnam launches military attacks against Cambodia. Pol Pot warmly welcomed in China.

January 1978   Sino-Vietnamese tensions rise regarding Vietnamese treatment of overseas Chinese in Vietnam.

June-July 1978   Beijing suspends aid to Vietnam; closes border to overseas Chinese fleeing Vietnam for refuge in China. Vietnam joins the Soviet bloc economic group, the Council for Mutual Economic Assistance.

October 1978   U.S.-Vietnamese talks on possible normalization of relations are suspended.

November 1978   Vietnam signs friendship treaty with U.S.S.R.

Dec. 15, 1978   U.S.-Chinese normalization of relations announced.

Dec. 25, 1978   Vietnamese troops invade Cambodia; take Phnom Penh by January 7; establish a new government for Cambodia.

Feb. 17, 1979   China begins limited military attack on northern Vietnam in order to "teach a lesson" to Hanoi.

March 1979   Soviet naval ships begin using Cam Ranh Bay.

June 1982   Sihanouk, Son Sann and the Khmer Rouge form the Coalition Government of Democratic Kampuchea (CGDK).

January 1985   U.S. Congress begins annual authorization of small amounts (around $5 million) of nonlethal aid to the noncommunist Cambodian resistance forces under Prince Sihanouk and Son Sann.

March 1985   Vietnamese troops destroy resistance base camps near Thai border in most aggressive dry season offensive along the border.

1986   CGDK introduces the notion of a four-party coalition government as part of a plan for a Cambodian peace settlement.

Aug. 10, 1987   U.S. envoy, General Vessey briefed President Reagan on his August 1-3, 1987 visit to Vietnam.

Sept. 11, 1987   The State Department announced that the United States and Vietnam had reached an agreement in principle to resettle Vietnamese children of American fathers.

Dec. 4, 1987   Prince Sihanouk ended three days of talks in France with Phnom Penh's prime minister Hun Sen.

August 1, 1988   Four days of peace talks on Cambodia ended in Indonesia.

Oct. 11, 1988   President Reagan met with noncommunist Cambodian leader Prince Sihanouk.

Dec. 22, 1988   Peace talks in Paris among the Cambodian factions broke up in discord.

Jan. 19, 1989   A Reagan administration report noted the difficulties involved in ever getting a full accounting of MIAs in Indochina.

Feb. 21, 1989   Talks on a Cambodian peace agreement among Indochinese and ASEAN representatives ended inconclusively.

Feb. 25, 1989   A humanitarian delegation of U.S. doctors left Vietnam after performing 100 operations on Vietnamese children.

Feb. 27, 1990   President Bush met with Prince Sihanouk in Beijing.

April 5, 1989   Vietnam announced that all of its troops would leave Cambodia by September 30, 1989.

May 1, 1989   Vice President Quayle met with Sihanouk in Indonesia.

May 3, 1989   Cambodian resistance leaders Sihanouk and Son Sann held talks in Indonesia with Phnom Penh regime leader Hun Sen.

June 7, 1989   A Japanese monk, released by Vietnam in January 1989 after 14 years, claimed that five or six U.S. POWs were still in captivity in Vietnam.

June 22, 1989   Responding to congressional criticism of the Bush administration's reported covert lethal aid program for Cambodia, Vice President Quayle called on Congress to publicly debate the administration's plan.

July 25, 1989   In Paris, Prince Sihanouk began another round of peace talks with the PRK's Hun Sen.

Aug. 30, 1989   An international conference in Paris failed in bridging differences among the Cambodian factions and their backers over a peace agreement.

Sept. 26, 1989   Vietnam hailed the "complete and final" withdrawal of its forces from Cambodia.

Oct. 22, 1989   Khmer Rouge forces claimed to have taken the town of Pailin, near the Thai border.

Oct. 30, 1989   General Vessey ended two days of talks in Hanoi.

Jan. 5, 1990   The State Department said that it hoped up to 7,000 former inmates in Vietnamese reeducation centers and their families would be relocated in the United States during FY1990.

Jan. 16, 1990   Talks on Cambodia among the five permanent members of the U.N. Security Council ended in Paris with an agreement on general principles.

Jan. 19, 1990   Moscow announced that some of its warplanes stationed at Cam Ranh airfield had returned to the Soviet Union in late 1989.

Feb. 18, 1990   Senator Robb held talks with Cambodian officials in Phnom Penh.

Feb. 22, 1990   The *New York Times* reported that several thousand Vietnamese military personnel had returned to Cambodia in late 1989 to help protect western Cambodian cities from insurgent attacks.

March 1, 1990   Peace talks in Jakarta among the Cambodian factions ended in failure.

March 13, 1990   Talks on Cambodia among the five U.N. Security Council permanent members ended in Paris.

April 12, 1990   Senator Kerrey began talks with Cambodian officials in Phnom Penh.

June 4, 1990   The Khmer Rouge walked out of peace talks in Tokyo between Sihanouk and Hun Sen.

June 27, 1990   The House approved continued overt aid to the noncommunist Cambodian resistance after a heated debate. The Senate Intelligence Committee reportedly voted to cut off covert aid to the noncommunist resistance.

July 17, 1990   The latest round of talks on Cambodia of the five U.N. Security Council permanent members ended in Paris.

July 18, 1990   Secretary Baker announced that the administration would seek contacts with Hanoi to reach a Cambodian settlement and would no longer support the three party coalition containing the Khmer Rouge in the United Nations.

July 29, 1990   After talks in Southeast Asia, Secretary of State Baker failed to secure the ASEAN foreign ministers' agreement with the recent shift in administration policy in Cambodia.

Aug. 6, 1990   U.S. and Vietnamese officials met in New York to discuss peace in Cambodia.

Sept. 9, 1990   The four Cambodian factions met in Indonesia to endorse a detailed peace plan approved in late August by the five permanent U.N. Security Council members. Concurrently, the U.S. government began official contacts with the Phnom Penh government.

Suggested Readings

Ackland, Len. *Vietnam: Unified, Independent and Poor.* Washington, Congressional Quarterly, 1988.

Americans Missing in Southeast Asia. Committee on Veteran's Affairs, U.S. House of Representatives, 100th Congress. Washington, G.P.O., 1988.

Anderson, Terry H. *The Light at the End of the Tunnel: The United States and the Socialist Republic of Vietnam.* Diplomatic History, Volume 12, Fall 1988.

Asia's Newest Profit Frontier. Business Tokyo, Volume 3, Summer 1989.

Asia Watch Committee (U.S.). *Khmer Rouge Abuses Along the Thai-Cambodian border.* Washington, D.C., available from Human Rights Watch, 1989.

Aspen Institute. *Indochina Policy Forum.* Recommendations for the New Administration on United States Policy Toward Indochina. Queenstown, MD, The Institute, 1988.

Bartu, Friedemann. *Between the Tiger and the Crocodile.* Swiss Review of World Affairs, Volume 38, August 1988.

Becker, Elizabeth. *The Progress of Peace in Cambodia.* Current History, Volume 88, April 1989.

_____. *When the War Was Over: The Voices of Cambodia's Revolution and Its People.* New York, 1986.

Bekaert, Jacques. *A Nasty Little War: Cambodia.* International Defense Review, Volume 22, March 1989.

Berlow, Alan. *Never Again? Cambodia: Still Haunted by the Khmer Rouge.* Harper's Magazine, Volume 279, October 1989.

Brown, Frederick Z. *Second Chance: The United States and Indochina in the 1990s.* New York, Council on Foreign Relations Press, 1989.

Brown, William A. *Indochinese Refugees and Relations with Thailand.* Washington, U.S. Department of State, 1988. Current Policy no. 1052.

Buszynski, Leszek. *The Concept of Political Regulation in Soviet Foreign Policy: The Case of the Kampuchean Issue.* Canberra, Strategic and Defence Studies Centre, Australian National University, 1989. Working Paper no. 182.

Cambodia Federation of American Scientists (F.A.S.). Public Interest Report, Volume 42, Washington, D.C., 1989.

Casella, Alexander. *The Refugees From Vietnam: Rethinking the Issue.* World Today, Volume 45, August-September 1989.

Chanda, Nayan. *Brother Enemy: The War After the War.* New York, 1986.

_____. *Cambodia in 1987: Sihanouk on Center Stage.* Asian Survey, Volume 28, January 1988.

_____. *Cambodia's Future: The View from Vietnam.* Madison, WI: Center for Southeast Asian Studies, University of Wisconsin, 1987.

_____. *Civil War in Cambodia?* Foreign Policy, no. 76, Fall 1989.

Chang, Pao-min. *Beijing, Hanoi, and the Overseas Chinese.* Institute of East Asian Studies. University of California, Berkeley, Center for Chinese Studies. 1982.

_____. *Kampuchea Between China, Vietnam and Sinapore.* Singapore, Singapore University Press, National University of Singapore, 1985.

Cima, Ronald J. *Vietnam's Economic Reform: Approaching the 1990s.* Asian Survey, Volume 29, August 1989.

Conboy, Kenneth J. *Dealing with a Fast Changing Indochina.* Washington Heritage Foundation, 1989. Asian Studies Center Backgrounder no. 87.

_____. *Washington Should Listen to its Friends and Take a More Active Role in Cambodia.* Washington, Heritage Foundation. 1989. Backgrounder no. 97.

Crossette, Barbara. *After the Killing Fields: Cambodia's Forgotten Refugees.* New York Times Magazine, sec. 6, June 26, 1988.

Davidson, Phillip B. *The History 1946-1975: Vietnam at War.* Novato, California, Presidio Press, 1988.

Duiker, William J. *China and Vietnam: The Roots of Conflict.* Berkeley: Institute of East Asian Studies, University of California, 1986.

_____. *Vietnam: The Challenge of Reform.* Current History, Volume 88, April 1989.

Erlanger, Steven. *The Return of the Khmer Rouge: The Endless War.* New York Times Magazine, March 5, 1989.

Esterline, John H. *Vietnam in 1987: Steps Toward Rejuvenation.* Asian Survey, Volume 28, January 1988.

Frieson, Kate. *The Political Nature of Democratic Kampuchea.* Pacific Affairs, Volume 61, Fall 1988.

Gaffney, Charles. *Vietnam: Some Glasnost in the Gloom?* Columbia Journalism Review, Volume 26, January-February 1988.

Greenway, H.D.S. *Report from Cambodia: The Tiger and the Crocodile.* New Yorker, Volume 65, July 17, 1989.

Hannum, Hurst. *International Law and Cambodian Genocide: The Sounds of Silence.* Human Rights Quarterly, Volume 11, February 1989.

Hiebert, Murray. *Cambodia.* Far Eastern Economic Review, Volume 143, January 12, 1989.

Immerman, Richard H. *The United States and the Geneva Conference of 1954: A New Look.* Diplomatic History, Volume 14, Winter 1990.

The Indochina Policy Forum (U.S.). *Indochina Policy Forum.* Queenstown, Md., Aspen Institute, 1988.

_____. *Recommendations for United States Policy Towards Cambodia.* The Aspen Institute, Washington, D.C., 1989.

Indo-Chinese Refugees and Asylum Seekers: Looking for New Solutions. Refugees, no. 65, June 1989.

Japan and the Problem of Kampuchea. Contemporary Southeast Asia, Volume 11, December 1989.

Kampuchea Problem: Solution is Near, Yet Far. World Focus, Volume 9, June 1988.

Kattenburg, Paul M. *The U.S. and Indochina: Then and Now.* Australian Outlook, Volume 42, August 1988.

Kelly, James A. *The United States in Southeast Asia: A Political-Security Agenda.* Washington Quarterly, Volume 12, Autumn 1989.

Kenny, Henry J. *The American Role in Vietnam and East Asia: Between Two Revolutions.* With a foreward by Mike Mansfield. New York, Praeger, 1984.

Kiernan, Ben. *How Pol Pot Came to Power: A History of Communism in Kampuchea, 1930-1975.* London, Verso, 1985.

_____. *Orphans of Genocide: The Cham Muslims of Kampuchea Under Pol Pot.* Bulletin of Concerned Asian Scholars, Volume 20, October-December 1988.

Kitchens, Allen H. *Normalizing U.S.-Vietnamese Relations.* In Essays on Strategy V. Washington, National Defense University Press, for sale by the Supt. of Docs., G.P.O., 1988.

Klintworth, Gary and Ross Babbage. *Peacekeeping in Cambodia: An Australian Role?* Canberra, Strategic and Defence Studies Centre. Australian National University, 1989. Working paper no. 179.

____. *The Vietnamese Achievement in Kampuchea.* Canberra, Strategic and Defence Studies Centre. Australian National University, 1989. Working paper no. 181.

Lawson, Eugene K. *The Sino-Vietnamese Conflict.* New York, Praeger, 1984.

LeBoutillier, John. *Coming to Terms with Vietnam.* New York Times magazine, May 1, 1988.

____. *Vietnam Now: A Case for Normalizing Relations with Hanoi.* Introduction by Richard M. Nixon; foreword by Liz Trotta. New York, Praeger, 1989.

Marr, David G. and Christine P. White. *Postwar Vietnam: Dilemmas in Socialist Development.* Ithaca, N.Y., Southeast Asia Program, Cornell University, 1988.

Marshall, Patrick G. *Cambodia's Never-ending Civil War.* Washington, Congressional Quarterly, 1989, volume 2, no. 11.

Martin, Richard. *Final Act in Long Kampuchean Tragedy?* Insight (Washington Times), volume 4, August 1, 1988.

____. *Inhabitants Live on Edge in Border Refugee Camps.* Insight (Washington Times), volume 4, August 1, 1988.

McAuliff, John and McDonnell, Mary Byrne. *Ending the Cambodian Stalemate.* World Policy Journal, volume 7, Winter 1989-90.

McGurn, William. *The Scandal of the Boat People.* Commentary, volume 89, January 1990.

Metzler, John J. *Vietnan's Admission to the United Nations: A Double-Edged Diplomatic Decision.* Issues & Studies, volume 24, February 1988.

Milivojevic, Marko. *The Spratly and Paracel Islands Conflict.* Survival, volume 31, January-February 1989.

Nossov, Mikhail G. *The USSR and the Security of Asia-Pacific Region: From Vladivostok to Krasnoyarsk.* Asian Survey, volume 29, March 1989.

Pike, Douglas. *The Cambodian Peace Process: Summer of 1989.* Asian Survey, volume 29, September 1989.

_____. *Vietnam's Foreign Relations, 1975-78.* CRS Report. Washington, G.P.O., 1979.

Porter, Gareth. *Cambodia: Sihanouk's Initiative.* Foreign Affairs, volume 66, Spring 1988.

_____. *Vietnam, A History in Documents.* New York, New American Library, 1981.

POW-MIA Fact Book. Washington, Department of Defense. 1989.
Refugeee Denied: Problems in the Protection of Vietnamese and Cambodians in Thailand and the Admission of Indochinese Refugees into the United States. New York, Lawyers Committee for Human Rights, 1989.

Ross, Robert S. *The Indochina Tangle: China's Vietnam Policy, 1975-1979.* New York, Columbia University Press, 1988.

Scalapino, Robert A. *Asia and the United States: The Challenges Ahead.* Foreign Affairs, volume 69, no. 1, 1990.

_____. *Sideshow: Kissinger, Nixon, and the Destruction of Cambodia.* New York, Simon and Schuster, 1979.

Sieng, Lapresse. *Cambodia: Twelve Years of Suffering.* International Freedom Review, volume 1, summer 1988.

Sigur, Gaston J. *Review of U.S.-Vietnamese Issues.* Washington, U.S. Department of State, Bureau of Public Affairs, 1988. Current Policy no. 1098

Snepp, Frank. *Decent Interval.* New York, Random House, 1977.

Sodhy, Pamela. *A Survey of U.S. Post-Vietnam Policy and the Kampuchean Dilemma, 1975-89: A Southeast Asian view.* Contemporary Southeast Asia, volume 11, December 1989.

Solomon, Richard H. *Cambodia and Vietnam: Trapped in an Eddy of History?* Washington, U.S. Department of State, Bureau of Public Affairs, 1989. Current Policy no. 1206

Son Sen. *"No More Revolutionary Ideals".* International Defense Review, volume 22, July 1989.

Stern, Lewis M. *Cambodia: Diplomacy Falters.* Current History, volume 89, March 1990.

_____. *The Vietnamese Communist Policy Toward the Overseas Chinese, 1983-1986.* Asian Profile, volume 16, April 1988.

Stone, Jeremy J. *U.S. Policy in Cambodia: All Wrong.* F.A.S. Public Interest Report, volume, 42, April 1989.

Sutter, Valerie. *The Indochinese Refugee Dilemma.* Baton Rouge, Louisiana State University Press, 1990.

Tasker, Rodney and Hiebert, Murray. *A Test of Arms.* Far Eastern Economic Review, volume 145, September 28, 1989.

Tonnesson, Stein. *Proposals for a Lasting Peace in Indochina.* Bulletin of Peace Proposals, volume 20, September 1989.

Twentieth Anniversary Issue on Indochina and the War. Bulletin of Concerned Asian Scholars, volume 21, April-December 1989.

Twining, Charles H. *Situation in Cambodia.* Department of State Bulletin, volume 88, December 1988.

U.S. Congress. House. Committee on Armed Services. Delegation to the Far East. *Report of the Delegation to the Far East of the Committee on Armed Services, House of Representatives.* Washington, G.P.O., 1988.

U.S. Congress. House. Committee on Foreign Affairs. *Cambodia After Five Years of Vietnamese Occupation.* Hearing and markup, 98th Congress, 1st Session on H. Con. Res. 176. Washington, G.P.O., 1983.

U.S. Congress. House. Committee on Foreign Affairs. Subcommittee on Foreign Affairs. Subcommittee on Asian and Pacific Affairs. *The Democratic Kampuchea Seat at the United Nations and American Interests.* Hearings, 97th Congress. Washington, G.P.O., 1983.

_____. *Kampuchea and American Foreign Policy Interests.* Hearing, 97th Congress, 1st Session. Washington, G.P.O., 1982.

_____. *1979 -- Tragedy in Indochina: War, Refugees, and Famine.* Hearing, 96th Congress, 1st Session. Washington, G.P.O., 1980.

_____. *U.S. Policy Toward Indochina Since Vietnam's Occupation of Kampuchea.* Hearing, 97th Congress, 1st Session. Washington, G.P.O., 1981.

U.S. Congress. House. Subcommittee on Asian and Pacific Affairs. *The Crisis Facing Vietnamese Refugees Seeking First Asylum in Thailand.* Hearing, 100th Congress, 2nd session. Washington, G.P.O., 1989.

_____. *Hope for Cambodia: Preventing the Return of the Khmer Rouge and Aiding the Refugees.* Hearing and markup, 100th Congress, 2nd Session on H.J. Res. 602. Washington, G.P.O., 1989.

_____. *The Implications of Establishing Reciprocal Interest Sections with Vietnam.* Hearing, 100th Congress, 2nd Session. Washington, G.P.O., 1989.

_____. *Indochinese Refugees at Risk: The Boat People, Cambodians under Khmer Rouge Control, and Re-education-Camp Detainees.* Hearing 101st Congress. 1st Session. Washington, G.P.O., 1989.

_____. *The Vessey Mission to Hanoi.* Hearing 100th Congress, 1st Session. Washington, G.P.O., 1988.

U.S. Congress. House. Committee on the Judiciary. *Categories of Soviet and Indochinese Presumed Subject to Persecution and Adjustment to Refugee Status of Certain Soviet and Indochinese Parolees.* Report, House, 101st Congress, 1st Session, No. 101-122. Washington, G.P.O., 1989.

U.S. Congress. House. Committee on the Judiciary. Subcommittee on Immigration, Refugees, and International Law. *Orderly Departure Program and U.S. Policy Regarding Vietnamese Boat People.* Hearing, 101st Congress, 1st Session. Washington, G.P.O., 1990.

U.S. Congress. House. Select Committee on Hunger. *Three Asian Countries in Crisis: Afghanistan, Vietnam, and The Philippines.* Hearing, 100th Congress, 2nd Session. Washington, G.P.O., 1988.

U.S. Senate. Committee on Foreign Relations. *Vietnam's Future Policies and Role in Southeast Asia.* Congressional Research Service, Library of Congress. Washington, G.P.O., 1982.

VanDerKroef, Justus M. *Cambodia: The Vagaries of "Cocktail" Diplomacy.* Contemporary Southeast Asia, volume 9, March 1988.

Vickery, Michael. *Kampuchea: Politics, Economics, and Society.* London, F. Pinter; Boulder, L. Rienner Publishers, 1986.

Vietnam. Military Review, volume 49, January 1989.

Weatherbee, Donald E. *Southeast Asia Divided: The ASEAN Indochina Crisis.* Boulder, Colorado, Westview Press, 1985.

Index